Dedication:

I dedicate this to my family, who never ceases to support and believe in me.

Thorns In My Garden

By R. A. Williams

Table of Contents

Introduction: 1
An Awakening 6
The What And The Why 10
The When 22
Repentance 26
Renovation 40
Briers And Thorns 55
The Who 66
Doorways 77
Deliverance In Scripture 82
Healing And Deliverance 87
The Where 92
Firsthand Deliverance 111
True Mercy 120
Christian Deliverance? 134
Intercession 142
How To Achieve Deliverance 145

INTRODUCTION:

I won't beat around the thornbush – you'll get that pun later – I've never met anyone who claimed to be an expert in spiritual warfare. Believe me, I've searched. And don't worry; I do NOT claim to be an expert either. The more I learn about God, the less I realize I know. I am sharing what little God has shared with me so far because I have greatly benefitted from this information.

My primary purpose in this journey with you is to bring awareness of a misconception that complete freedom is an automatic by-product of receiving the Holy Ghost. I spent over thirty years bound by spirits and generational curses I was told I could not have while also having the Holy Ghost. If you disagree with this concept, you are too late to convince me otherwise. Scriptures, together with my personal experiences, far outweigh any arguments. At this point, my responsibility for sharing what God has given me is more important than what anyone else, who knows me, might think of me. (Matthew 16:24, 25) My intentions are simple; I want someone else to experience freedom as I have.

Freedom often requires a battle, and thus the ominous term "spiritual warfare." Jesus is our victory. He has created all things, and He is the ultimate authority. (Psalms 24:1; Matthew 28:18; John 1:1-3, 10-17; Colossians 1:16-20; 2:10; 1 Peter 3:22)

If you are hungry for more of God, like I am, or tired of fighting certain feelings or invasive thoughts like I was, this is for you.

I wouldn't encourage anyone to jump into a ring with an enemy they know nothing about, so there will be a practical foundation for spiritual warfare before we dive into the basics of deliverance.

I will share personal experiences that might be troubling, especially for those new to the Lord. If you find any information uncomfortable, pray about it; you may not be ready to receive this knowledge yet, and that's okay. My goal is not to create fear but to create awareness which I feel is lacking in today's generation. I understand that I am held accountable to the Lord for my words, and in no way have any of these personal instances been embellished or fabricated.

Since this topic concerns the darker side of spiritual warfare, I will not have equal information about God's angelic host. This does not minimize their significant role in the spirit realm or warfare in any way. My goal is to give awareness about our enemy because much of the information this generation is getting about that subject doesn't come from the church. Also, I want to clarify upfront; I do not intend to give our adversary any unnecessary credit. The enemy does not have equal opposite power as Jesus. There is no opposite for Jesus. He is the eternal Creator and far above any created being.

By the end of this journey, we will have answered the following questions: *What* is spiritual warfare? *Why* do we experience spiritual warfare? *When* should we engage in spiritual warfare? *How* do we engage in spiritual warfare? *Who* needs deliverance? *Who* should participate in deliverance? *Where* exactly does deliverance happen? And finally, *How* can deliverance be accomplished?

(Any original O.T. Hebrew or N.T. Greek translations and definitions for understanding enhancement will be found in italics inside these brackets {} within scripture for less confusion and easier comprehension. Outside of scripture text, each term will be <u>underlined</u> with its definition in italics. All Bible and translation references used throughout are from TouchBible K.J.V. + Strong's App[1])

I will begin with how the Lord inspired my journey and then provide the insight I received along the way. Most importantly, there will be scripture references for each revelation with a Bible study-type format for specific points. Each previous question will be underlined along with its answer. I will finish with an example of a deliverance prayer on pg. 149. This type of prayer has helped me and others to acquire more freedom.

I want to establish additional disclaimers to prevent any misunderstandings: I do NOT believe that every ailment, disability, syndrome, or circumstance is spiritual. Because my focus here is entirely on *spiritual* aspects, I want to avoid over-spiritualization or the absence of *common sense*. The spiritual angle does not lessen

---

[1]*Touch Bible (KJV + Strong's) App* (Version/Update 2019) [Mobile App] Patrick Franklin source Information:
https://www.touchbible.com
(This will be the only source location for all references with this number. I used apps from the App Store for Apple devices and Google Play for Android devices)

the importance of the practical and mortal aspects of our lives. I cannot stress how *crucial* common sense is, but at the same time, it is imperative to keep a level of sensitivity for the things of God. BALANCE IS EVERYTHING.

Unfortunately, to the average Christian in the U.S.A., spiritual warfare and deliverance are taboo subjects. There is an extreme lack of information from credible sources. Maybe it has been miscommunicated or misrepresented by people who were considered odd or unbalanced. Maybe Christians as a whole have been trying to avoid any unnecessary negative stereotypes. Whatever the reason, I'm sure our adversary relishes our lack of knowledge and apprehension on such a topic. But if we do not talk about it, who will? Do we want the next generation equipped with the *world's* view and definition of supernatural?

The growing population of those experimenting with the supernatural lets us know there are hungry and desperate people out there. At the same time, it's not a coincidence that depression and anxiety are on the rise globally. The growth of technology has undoubtedly contributed to our circumstances. Every type of information is at our fingertips. Now more than ever, it's time to replace the terrifying propaganda of the enemy with truth, peace, and freedom.

In His hour, Jesus' deliverance ministry ruffled the feathers of the religious people. It was untraditional and unconventional. There were many misconceptions concerning that ministry, yet crowds followed him and even took extreme measures to get deliverance. The first step beyond tradition and the unknown was no doubt challenging, but those desperate and hungry for more did not care. It seems much the same today; deliverance is misunderstood, unpredictable, and not at all glamorous. It requires sensitivity, compassion, and correct motives. If you really love God and people, you will not condemn deliverance. It is Jesus' ministry.

The following information is not meant to create a rigid mindset controlled by fear or obedience based on consequences. Some agendas have attached that stigma to *religion* as a whole. This is not about religion, tradition, or rules. This is about spiritual law, a deeper relationship with Jesus, and, most of all, *freedom.*

CHAPTER 1
AN AWAKENING

One morning I heard a minister encouraging his listeners to ask God for more understanding in the spirit realm. I wondered why I had never thought to ask that before, so I did. God answered immediately, "No, you are not ready." I didn't expect that, but I trusted that it was true.

My husband, a minister, and I served in youth ministry for over 20 years until changing paths a few years ago. His favorite part of that ministry has continued, which is altar working. My true hunger has always been for intercessory prayer. To be more effective, I wanted a deeper understanding of that whole aspect.

Our family faced some difficult trials a year after I prayed for more insight. I then understood why God had previously said that I was not ready. I had some secret impurities that surfaced through those trials, and ultimately those impurities needed to go. While waiting for more understanding, I allowed God to remove things that could not go with me to the next level. My prayer, Bible study, giving, and fasting increased. In the fall, a few years later, I felt a season of repentance, and I continued asking God to reveal my hidden faults and flaws. I felt like there was a spiritual door I could not enter until obstacles were removed. This season lasted for several months, and in January of the following year, the Lord gave me a vivid night vision.

I took this troubling vision to the Lord in prayer the next day but could not get any answers. I have learned over the years that if I don't get a response after 45 minutes to an hour in prayer, He will reveal what I need to know in time. (In Chapter 3, "The When," I will mention a little more about dreams.)

The understanding was not there yet for me to receive the revelation. God knew, in a few short months, I would need the insight that He had already provided. My traditional mindset was an obstacle because I had always been taught that evil spirits could only be *around* but not *attached to/inside* someone who had the Holy Ghost.

A few weeks after the night vision, I was told by a friend to check out a certain minister online. It was not a coincidence that his current message was about renouncing. I had never heard a message about renouncing and thought it couldn't hurt to try. In this season of repentance and hunger for more of God, my curiosity was especially piqued.

Since I was alone at home, I began renouncing everything that came to mind. I renounced old sins from before conversion that I had never mentioned specifically in prayer. I renounced the sins of my ancestors and the things with which I struggled. I was probably renouncing for about fifteen minutes when suddenly, as I repented and renounced selfishness, I realized I was shaking my head no. I felt resistance in my spirit and continued pushing forward against selfishness. At that point, in my years of living for God, I had only encountered resistance a few times in my own prayer time. However, I had experienced resistance during the deliverance of others several times. Those experiences helped me recognize that the resistance I was now feeling was from the enemy. I instantly saw a vision of myself as a child and heard the word "timidity." (I distinctly remember being outgoing as a small child but became shy after an incident in grade school.) I saw the actual moment when these two spirits (that I had never considered to be spirits) came upon me. I then asked God's help in removing these spirits from me, and with His help, I took authority and commanded them to leave. At first, it felt as if something began unraveling from my spine, and after a little while, I felt a complete release. When my husband returned home later, he remarked how he noticed something different about me (in a good way.)

Once selfishness and timidity were exposed by renouncing and then removed, the other attachments were revealed. Most of these attachments were what I had always considered to be character flaws or personality traits, but they were more than that. Timidity was a partner to selfishness, which resulted in continuous insecurity. Those attachments did not necessarily control me but instead tormented and distracted me. Getting ready to go places, I would have to listen to music or something to drown out the intrusive thoughts in my mind. If I didn't, I would hear every negative thing ever said about me or my looks. I dreaded new or uncomfortable social settings because of the continual negative chatter that invaded my thoughts. Things like: 'No one will want to talk to you, you will probably do or say the wrong thing,' etc. After most social interactions, my thoughts were bombarded with a constant replay of every negative thing that happened. Most of the thoughts were about *me* failing in some way. If the social obligation ended at night, I would have trouble sleeping because, in the quiet, those continuous replays were even louder in my head. Overthinking was an understatement. Once I was delivered, all of that stopped immediately. Of course, I still have an occasional thought in reflection of something I have said that didn't make sense, which is completely normal, but it is nothing like the previous tormenting circumstances.

After that deliverance, I had to work on the stronghold of YEARS of shy *behavior*. The thoughts were gone, but my default for most of my life had been timid. I had to consciously make an effort to override that default daily until my new habitual behavior was no longer shy. These were not terrifying spirits that would make for good horror stories. Nothing about the deliverance was scary. The worst part was the shame I felt and my lack of knowledge. I honestly think there is an agenda aimed toward fear of this subject to keep us bound. My timidity was a considerable obstacle in every area of my life and ministry, tormenting my mind, dissolving peace, attacking my faith and health, and creating significant barriers that prevented me from helping and reaching others.

<u>2 Timothy 1:7</u> "For God hath not given us the spirit of fear; but of power, and of love, and of a sound mind."

"Fear" here is a Greek term used only once: 1167 <u>*deilia*</u> – *timidity*[1] referencing 1169 <u>*deilos*</u> – *faithless.*[1] (The most common terms used for "fear" in the New Testament are 5399 <u>*phobeo*</u>[1] and 5401 <u>*phobos*</u>.[1] Those last terms are where we get the English word phobia.)

Experiencing deliverance gave me a new outlook, much like the eye-opening experience when I received the Holy Ghost years before. It also gave me clarity on some instances that happened in previous years. After I encountered some opposition from other Christians about this new revelation, I cried out to the Lord in prayer. The Lord reminded me of the night vision I had a few weeks prior and began to give me the interpretation, insight, and, most importantly, scriptures.

Deliverance didn't end there, however. This personal story will be continued in Chapter 12, "Firsthand Deliverance." In the next chapters, I will lay a foundation and provide the answers and the scriptures that God has given me. The journey into more freedom didn't end with one deliverance for me; it had just begun.

CHAPTER 2
THE WHAT AND THE WHY

What is spiritual warfare? Spiritual warfare is a battle with mostly unseen forces of opposition from the spirit realm. This battle usually affects our natural realm as well. Some consider all resistance to be spiritual warfare, but I do not want to give the enemy that much credit. It is not healthy to consider ourselves always being bullied by the enemy.

Spiritual warfare in deliverance is opposition when dealing with freedom from an evil spirit, unclean spirit, demon, devil, oppression, possession, curse, or whichever term applies. "Attachments" is an easier blanket term, and it sounds less fear-provoking.

Our natural man is not equipped to fight in the spirit realm. The disciplines of prayer, fasting, Bible study, faithfulness, worship, praise, submission, and self-control are our weapons against the enemy. There are also the aspects of soul-winning and deliverance that significantly weaken the enemy. We must not attempt spiritual warfare on our own. Any entrance into the spirit realm, except through Jesus, is dangerous and presumptuous.

My understanding began with the first deliverance alone with just me and God, thirteen years after receiving the Holy Ghost, although I didn't understand it was deliverance at that time. Maybe this will help someone who has possibly battled with the same issue:

Years ago, I battled with hopelessness. That seed was planted as I began revisiting memories from my past. I preferred thinking of my past because it was my happy place. In reality, those memories were an escape that fed my pride. *Foundations or motives of pride and vanity are destructive.* (Proverbs 16:18; 18:12, Also, in the descriptions of Lucifer - Isaiah 14:13, 14; Ezekiel 28:17; 1 Peter 5:5) I became bound to a reflection mindset but noticed when I fasted, the thought pattern loosened its hold. It was such a deceptive spirit that I was completely unaware I was bound by a spirit. I was deceived into thinking those thoughts and feelings were my own. I was convinced I would always feel that way. My red flag was that my feelings and thoughts didn't align with scripture, which was also confusing because I had God's Spirit inside me. I was sincere in my relationship with God and kept a consistent prayer life. I studied the Bible, fasted, attended church regularly, and had strong convictions, but... I had not taken every thought captive. (Philippians 4:8; 2 Corinthians 10:5) I was a one God, Apostolic, tongue talking, tithe paying, modest dresser, so I must be okay, I thought. The truth is we can be covered head to toe and pray in tongues while having sin in our hearts. I was involved in church leadership in several areas, and it was evident that His power would move at times in the ministry with which the Lord had entrusted me.

God will pour out of whoever is available. He does this for the sake of others. We can be a vessel when we are at the right place and right time, in spite of us, not because of us. Even if God is flowing through us, in the gifts of the Spirit, laying hands on the sick, praying people through, casting out devils, or praying in tongues, none of that is the super stamp of approval that we are sin free.

I was done feeling hopeless, so one afternoon, I attempted what is now commonly known as *self*-deliverance. (Could Matthew 7:3-5 be suggesting this?) I started out praying the most sincere and desperate prayer of repentance. Then following the direction of the Holy Ghost, I felt to speak to the evil spirit that was tormenting me. This was entirely unconventional for me because, at the time, I had never heard anyone say if Christians, who were not ministers, should *speak* to an evil spirit. The whole process took a while, and I had to stop at times and praise the Lord as I got weary. I prayed until I then felt Holy Ghost authority come over me, and my tongue/prayer language changed to a different language that seemed very authoritative. (I have since heard deliverance ministers instruct only to speak the native language of the individual being delivered because it is important that the evil spirit understands its orders.) I just followed God because I had no idea how to cast out/off an evil spirit by myself, even though I had seen it done several times. I put my hand on my head and commanded whatever it was to leave while speaking in the authoritative language; it left! I had no knowledge of the concept at the time, but I felt strongly about sending it to the "pit." I experienced coughing and gagging while praying and then visibly saw it depart from me at eye level. Once the evil spirit left, I was instantly relieved. I wasn't sure if the coughing and gagging were from crying. It is possible, but I cried and prayed often and rarely if ever, felt that. God then told me that He had given me spiritual authority in the area that I had just overcome. I rationalized that I must have been oppressed but wasn't sure what that really meant. I had always thought it meant an attack from the outside, and this spirit felt as if it had left from inside of me. We will further explore this subject in Chapter 11, "The Where."

Praise is a critical part of the process. Praising Jesus allows Him to refuel you with His strength. (I remembered this from one of several messages I have heard Reverend Billy Cole preach over the years.) After I rested, I realized my mind didn't reflect along its usual train of thought! My mind had been wholly and instantly delivered! I imagined that the neuropathway of those habitual thoughts had closed completely! For several days, I checked my thought pattern every morning to ensure it was still gone and was careful not to cultivate those thoughts any longer.

As odd as this all sounds, I wanted answers to where this spiritual attachment had been. It crept into my mind through the thoughts I had allowed. There are so many Biblical terms to express the concepts of our inner man, such as the words used for the "mind." The most common Hebrew terms for "mind" are 05315 *nephesh – soul*,[1] (07307 *ruwach – spirit*,[1] and 03820 *lev/leb – heart*.[1] Greek terms: 1271 *dianoia – thoughts, feelings, mind, understanding, spirit*,[1] and 3563 *nous – intellect, understanding, and perception*.[1] Greek for "soul" is 5590 *psyche* meaning *breath, spirit, immortal soul, heart-mind, affections, feelings*,[1] Greek for "heart" is 2588 *kardia* meaning *heart, mind, emotions, desires, center of all physical and spiritual life*.[1]

So, using one technical term to determine exactly what part of the inner man is affected by certain sins is difficult, especially if the words in the Bible are used interchangeably. Jesus touches on each of these terms in Matthew 22:37. If using the definitions from the Greek translations; it appears we are supposed to love the Lord with all our thoughts/intellect, emotions/feelings, and desires/being. It is sobering to think that even the way we live can be seen as worship. During prayer, the Lord reminded me recently that how we dress is part of our worship. That was so powerful to me! Modesty, covering, and gender distinction have a deeper meaning. Every sacrifice we make does not go unnoticed by the Lord and often by the enemy.

Satan lost his position in the Kingdom of God, and it seems this resulted from his pride, vanity, and thinking himself to be like God (Isaiah 14:12-17; Ezekiel 28:12-19.) There is controversy among Bible scholars about whether these scriptures are actually concerning Satan. Scriptures often had parallel meanings. Kings and nations were often compared to the principalities that dominated those kingdoms. The man – Prince of Tyrus, reflected the very attributes of pride as seen in Ezekiel 28:1-10. Verses 13 and 14 mention him being in the garden of Eden and an anointed cherub, which seems to imply Satan. Both the books of Daniel and Ezekiel suggest that principalities are assigned to territories. We should keep this in mind when considering the struggles of others. A pastor who judges another pastor from a different location must remember he is not being fought by the same principality.

The first appearance of opposition in the Garden of Eden was a serpent that disputed God's word and, in the disguise of "enlightenment," deceived Eve. This resulted in Adam and Eve disobeying God in eating the forbidden fruit in Genesis 3:1-7. Sin and death then entered humanity literally and spiritually. Ecclesiastes 7:20, Romans 3:10, 23, and 1 John 1:8-10 are scriptures that inform us that we are ALL born into sin. The first curse is mentioned in Genesis 3:14-19. This is a bloodline curse for all humanity. In Verse

15, the parallel of spiritual and physical opposition is spoken into existence.

Spiritual warfare took a dark turn briefly in Genesis 6:2. This passage mentions that the sons of God took wives of the daughters of men. Because there is so little information concerning this, there is a theory that this produced a combination of angelic/human *hybrids*, which is seen in Verse 4 as giants. The Hebrew word used for "giants" (05303 *Nphiyl*)[1] is used in what seems to be the plural form (*Nephilim.*)[1] It is connected to the word "05307 *Naphal – to fall, lie, be cast down, fail.*"[1] The same word is used for "fallen" in Isaiah 14:12, in the description of Lucifer.

Three verses after giants are mentioned in Genesis, God decides to destroy the earth and all wickedness. Interestingly, 2 Peter 2:4, 5 speaks of the sinning of angels and then the great flood in the next verse. Jude, Verse 6, also supports this idea. Could this event be where multiple evil spirits originated from the angel/human hybrids? Or will these deceased hybrid beings remain asleep or held captive with angels that left their first estate and sinned until judgment? Another possibility of evil spirit origin is seen in Revelation 12:4, 9, indicating that one-third of the angels followed Satan. To begin with, it seems no way to know exactly how many angels there are, so one-third of the angels could be the evil spirits that battle believers. Either way, we are aware of evil spirits that oppose us. I will add that no spirits from deceased humans, such as our relatives, remain as ghosts haunting the earth. (Ecclesiastes

9:3-6; 12:7; 1 Thessalonians 4:13-18; Hebrews 9:27; Revelation 20:12-14) In the account of 1 Samuel 28:3-19, notice that the woman used a familiar spirit to "bring up" Samuel. It implies in Verse 13 that he wasn't the only thing she "brought up." She used the lowercase "g" for "gods," to describe what she saw *ascending* out of the *earth*, which is the same word used in the definition of the Greek word for "demon." It is dangerous to use divination to contact the "dead." It is possible that "Samuel" in these verses was actually a familiar spirit posing as Samuel. Regardless of whether Samuel awakened or not, we are instructed not to try and contact the dead. (Leviticus 19:31; Deuteronomy 18:10; 2 Kings 17:17)

Further insight into our enemy continues with John 12:31, which mentions the prince of this world. Ephesians 2:2 speaks of the prince and power of the air, or in Greek, the ruler and authority of the atmospheric region. Satan "assumed" worldly kingdom authority in Luke 4:5-7. In John 8:44, he is referred to as a murderer and the father of lies, and then a deceiver, as we remember from Genesis and see in 2 Corinthians 11:14. In Revelation 12:10, Satan is described as the "accuser of our brethren." 1 Peter 5:8 gives a description: "....your adversary the devil, as a roaring lion, walketh about, seeking whom he may devour:" The Greek word for "adversary" here is "476 *antidikos* – an opponent in a lawsuit."[1] Satan looks for legal evidence against us.

<u>The enemy targets God's *Word* and *people*</u>. (Genesis 3:1-5, 15) The enemy attacks God's words. When the spiritual Kingdom of

God began to be born in new believers of Jesus, we started understanding the fragment of the Lord's Prayer that states in Matthew 6:10, "Thy kingdom come. Thy will be done in earth, as *it is* in heaven." There is a simultaneous battle – one we can sometimes see here on Earth and one we usually can't see in Heaven. The enemy does not like losing those who belong to his kingdom. When we were in darkness, we were not a threat. The more time we spend in God's Word, prayer, and fasting, the more we will come onto the enemy's radar. Fear of becoming a target is not of God. Jesus has all power. However, if the enemy can entice us to commit and remain in sin, he has a legal open door for defilement. (John 8:34)

<u>*Why*</u> do we even experience spiritual warfare? As you saw in the previous story, <u>sin</u> was the cause of *my* battle. Sometimes though, we experience warfare without sin. <u>The following list includes the seven most common reasons we can experience spiritual warfare.</u>

<u>Reasons We Can Feel Under Attack</u>:

1. <u>Sin</u>: If sin is present or through legal rights of a generational curse, this opens us to demonic attack. (Romans 6:16, 20) Repentance is necessary for forgiveness. Various aspects of repentance: Confession in certain circumstances to trustworthy people helps with accountability, but confession to God is most important; Renouncing is a more formal, detailed form of repentance from a legal perspective. Retracting is withdrawing negative words.

>Repentance: Luke 13:3; Acts 2:38
>Confession: James 5:16; 1 John 1:9
>Renouncing: 2 Corinthians 4:2

2. <u>Distraction</u>: The enemy seems to sense when we are about to have an opportunity, open door, or victory, and he will do everything he can to cause us to lose focus or be hindered from God's purpose. <u>Ask God for direction and to help you discern and overcome distractions</u>.

3. <u>Purify/Promotion</u>: God will sometimes allow an attack bringing to light something that needs to be removed from our life. Something that is holding us back from moving forward to the next level. Specific attacks are common to certain types of ministries. Example: Jezebel (bully, witchcraft, false prophecy) – Elijah (prophetic, intercessor). Also, God may want to anoint you in this area or produce a ministry out of your misery. The attack you overcome could be the armor that equips you for the future. Sometimes it is to bring judgment on the enemy to give you freedom and new authority. <u>Ask God to reveal in prayer the flaws that are holding you back and for sensitivity to His voice so that you can allow Him to work on you</u>. No one wants to experience a trial to reveal impurities or to keep repeating a test until they learn the lesson. <u>Ask God to show you what you need to know without a test</u>.

4. <u>Sensitivity</u>: Sometimes, what feels like an attack is a new heightened level of sensitivity in the spirit realm, and the believer is picking up on spirits that are around, or attached to people around them, etc. One obvious indication of this type of attack is suddenly dealing with something the believer usually doesn't have a problem with or has never struggled with. <u>Ask the Lord for discernment, wisdom, and understanding in this situation</u>. A more extreme case of this is typical of those with prophetic ministries. Many

Old Testament prophets literally lived a fleshly parallel to the spirit realm concerning their ministry. (Isaiah 20:2,3; Jeremiah's Lamentations; Hosea 1:2-11) Those prophets encountered turmoil and difficult living conditions but not because of their sin. It was for the sins of the country or people to which those prophets were sent.

5. <u>People</u>: Specific attacks on the mind, such as confusion, anxiety, discouragement, depression, and hopelessness, are characteristics of an attack of witchcraft against the believer. I have seen this happen when fellow believers speak openly and negatively *against* another person. This also could come in the form of some well-meaning person praying their own will or convictions on the believer. ALWAYS examine your motives in prayer so that you do not make this mistake, because regardless, we reap what we sow, so the amount of mercy and compassion you use in your words or prayer will return. If the motive for the prayer isn't founded in God's love, mercy, and perfect will, it could be a form of witchcraft. <u>If you feel this is happening to you, ask God to block any prayers *against* you</u>. The enemy would love to partner with other human beings to target you if possible. <u>Pray mercy and understanding toward those who might target you</u>.

6. <u>Progress</u>: If the believer has done an extended fast, experienced a victory, or made an advancement for the Lord's Kingdom through deliverance or soul-winning, the enemy will try to discourage breakthroughs, freedom, or revelation. He likes to remain hidden and work secretly for as long as possible. The enemy's goal is to prevent any further progress. If you are in any way causing problems for his kingdom, he will most likely respond with a counterattack. So, don't be surprised if you are under attack while taking territory from the enemy. He most likely will not stand by and watch you destroy his hard work without a hostile response. Jesus experienced this. (Matthew 4:1) -<u>We counteract this with God's</u>

<u>Word, canceling the enemy's assignments, blocking, and binding those counterattacks and demonic retaliation.</u>

7. <u>Picking a fight, especially with a principality, that you have not been authorized to fight</u>: There is much controversy on this topic, and it is strictly meant as a cautionary statement. (2 Peter 2:10-12; Jude, Verses 8-10) Jesus has all power over the enemy, and if we have His Spirit, we also have access to that same power; however, I have felt strongly for some time to take authority only when the Lord instructs me to do so. This idea is also implied in 2 Corinthians 10:13, 17, 18. <u>Ask the Lord for His permission to go into battle and await His response. Ask for authority and guidance according to His will.</u>

It is common for the enemy to use distractions before breakthroughs. I have experienced situations that provoked me to anger, and after a quick prayer for temperance, I found the Lord dealing with the very person that caused the anger. Suddenly there was an opportunity to reach them, which wouldn't have happened if I had given in to anger. Several times, I have discreetly gone to a nearby private place, often a restroom, and whispered (because apparently, spirits have good hearing) *binding* the enemy that was causing division. Afterward, I would *loose* unity and peace. *Every* time that situation immediately turned around.

Have you ever noticed a random person repeating the exact words the enemy has whispered into your mind? It wasn't the actual person that thought of those hurtful words. If the adversary planted thoughts and words to use someone against us, the adversary could use us if we let him. Often the enemy is also targeting an area in our life for a reason. Maybe there is a future ministry in this area or an anointing we are unaware of yet. As mentioned in Ephesians 4:26, 27, "Be ye angry, and sin not: let not the sun go down upon your wrath: Neither give place to the devil." The devil looks for an opportunity in our anger.

One morning after waking, a person I rarely think of was on my mind in a negative way. I wanted to discuss this person's situation with my husband but instead ignored the thoughts and remained silent. Later that day, I found out that person was having great difficulty, and I realized if I had negatively uttered the thoughts that the enemy had planted in my mind, I would have come into agreement with the enemy and spoken into the atmosphere the very words he wanted to be spoken. That is why it is important to take our thoughts captive to decide which thoughts are planted by the enemy, which are our own, and which are from God. I do not want to come into agreement with anything that the enemy has spoken. That is what we do when we say negative or harmful words that can hurt others.

Sometimes the enemy initiates an attack to provoke us to sin so that he can gain legal rights on our *property*. If the enemy overplays his hand, there is a day when enough is enough with God. An attack can suddenly bring our case before God as our righteous Judge, and if we are innocent, it can advance us spiritually. (2 Samuel 16:5-13; 19:16-23)

CHAPTER 3
THE WHEN

The next question isn't aimed at the aspect of deliverance but instead answers an essential question in *all* spiritual warfare. *When* do we engage in spiritual battles?

There is important insight concerning battle found in Numbers 14:26-45. In Verses 40 and 44, most of the children of Israel were determined to go to battle, despite Moses' warning in Verses 41-43. (Deuteronomy 1:19-45) Their previous lack of faith resulted in murmuring, pride, and disobedience, which caused them to lose the battle because the Lord's presence did not go with them. However, in contrast, we see in 1 Samuel 23:1-5 that David inquired of the Lord before his battle. He diligently sought the Lord's counsel even in the details, as seen in Verses 10-12. (1 Samuel 30:8; 2 Samuel 2:1; 2 Samuel 5:19, 23-25) Those battles were all successful because David asked the Lord before engaging.

I have found that engaging in a spiritual battle that we have not been authorized to fight is dangerous. We must seek the Lord before making alliances or commitments or if we are asked by another person to engage in a spiritual battle. It is also wise to ask the Lord to be our Counselor each new day.

I remember encountering a situation a few years ago in a very severe and delicate matter. In my humanness, I wanted to address the person making wrongful accusations toward my family member, but God prevented me. He had given me a dream several days before the situation transpired. In the dream, a large snake bit my finger when I pointed at the person involved in the real-life accusation. God stopped me just before I sent the text and reminded me of that dream. He told me that if I said something, I would provoke more damage. I was not authorized in this matter. I gave it to Him, and He handled it, but it had been very tempting to counterattack verbally. Looking back now, I can see the immense possibilities of damage that could have resulted, and I am so thankful for the Lord's guidance on that issue.

The Lord has admonished me in the category of dreams, that sometimes the issues conveyed in dreams are things He is warning me to pray *against*. They aren't always inevitable; I need to seek Him about them. I try to write my dreams down and pray about them, especially dreams with recurrent people or themes. Jesus has given me wisdom from dreams, and usually, if I give my prayer time to Him, allowing Him to lead me in prayer about what is on *His agenda first*, the Lord will then reveal the dream's meaning. We need to be careful about consulting even the Christian dream dictionaries because often, what something symbolizes to us might not have the same meaning to another.

For instance, I often dream of pets when God is trying to speak to me about loved ones because, as an only child growing up, pets were like family and friends. However, if you've had a negative experience with an animal that is normally a pet, dreaming of that animal might indicate a warning for you. Also, dreaming of predator-type creatures usually represents possible attacks. Pay attention to its characteristics.

The more vivid the dream, the more I pray about it, especially if it bothers me throughout the day. I am careful not to assume meanings about dreams or visions, though. I have often been deep in prayer, and the Lord reveals a meaning contrary to the definition I would've interpreted myself. It was amazing how I would have been completely off on the interpretation. I have asked the Lord to warn me in dreams, and thankfully He has many times.

There are two other places dreams can originate: our subconscious and the enemy. Our brains are processing events when we sleep. That is our body's way of working through things, so it is not wise to make a serious decision based on one dream. Usually, God will speak to us in a dream while also dealing with us about that subject in other ways. A dream from Jesus will never contradict scripture.

It is surprising how often God used dreams to speak to someone in the Bible. (Genesis 41; Daniel 2; Matthew 1:20; 2:12-22)

When we engage in a spiritual battle without the Lord's authorization, we risk being presumptuous and self-willed like those mentioned in Numbers 14:44 and 2 Peter 2:10-12. When we sin and overlook repenting of that sin, we become a target for the enemy. It may not be visible in our fleshly state but be sure it is visible in the spirit realm. I'm so thankful that Jesus paid the price for our sins! We have all atonement through the blood of Jesus! We must apply that to our lives. Each person's sins are not magically removed just because Jesus shed His blood for them. Each of us must come into agreement with His redemption through repentance, baptism in Jesus' Name, and receive the infilling of the Holy Ghost. God has all power, authority, and glory. My answer to the question of: <u>*When* do we engage in spiritual warfare? When God has authorized and called us into battle</u>.

Understanding that we cannot assume authority without God's prompting is essential. However, we can appeal to the Lord about situations. We may not have authority over the spiritual aspects of certain situations, but we can ask God to step in and take over.

If there is warfare concerning our own deliverance, it is appropriate to ask a spiritual leader in our lives to aid in our deliverance. If that is not possible, God is able to lead each of us through deliverance. If someone isn't comfortable or doesn't feel successful attempting deliverance by themselves, I suggest finding another trusted believer, preferably one called to deliverance ministry. Humility and willingness to be vulnerable before another may be the key. If a manifestation is hindering during self-deliverance, it could be easier to get freedom with the help of another. Unity is powerful. I also recommend seeking the Lord about the deliverance in prayer and fasting beforehand.

CHAPTER 4
REPENTANCE

Repentance has always been a precursor to a greater level. If I feel stuck in a spiritual traffic jam, it could be that my spiritual road is under construction. A new spiritual level is about to open that sometimes only repentance can unlock. Often, I have been guilty of hastily rushing through repentance in prayer, being very general, and hurrying on to what I think are the more urgent topics. However, there is a level of repentance that should not be overlooked, especially when one engages in warfare. It can only be found through waiting in God's presence and asking Him to reveal flaws inside of us.

"Repent ye…" was John the Baptist's ministry message preparing the way for Jesus, in Matthew 3:1-3. According to Acts 2:38, it was the first word Peter spoke when answering the multitude after their monumental question, "….what shall we do?"

Repentance is commonly connected with the term "altar," a place of sacrifice, *covenant*, and a transaction point symbolizing an ending and a new beginning.

Genesis 8:20-22 tells of Noah building an altar unto the Lord upon exiting the ark. When the Lord received his offerings, it resulted in a covenant from the Lord and a reversal of a previous curse from Genesis 3:17, 18, as God decided no longer to curse the ground for man's sake. (Note for future reference: Genesis 3:18 is the first mention of the term "thorns.")

Abram/Abraham built altars during significant moves or encounters with the Lord in Genesis 12:7, 8; 13:18; 22:9. Isaac and Jacob built altars during life-changing seasons in Genesis 26:25; 33:20 (Elelohe-Israel) and in 35:1-7 (Elbethel). Moses built and named an altar Jehovahnissi in Exodus 17:15 after a significant battle with Amalek. In Exodus 24:4, we see another built before a covenant and an encounter with the Lord. The Lord gave specific instructions for building an altar in Exodus 20:24-26, but in Exodus 27:1-8, the Lord gives instructions to build an altar that would be portable. Deuteronomy 27:1-8 mentions an altar after crossing Jordan. After a battle against Ai, Joshua built an altar in Joshua 8:30, 31. An altar named Ed was created for a witness or testimony by the tribes of Reuben, Gad, and the half-tribe of Manasseh in Joshua 22:10, 24-28, 34. Gideon built an altar in Judges 6:24-32 and called it Jehovahshalom. Then Manoah, the father of Samson, offered upon a rock unto the LORD in Judges 13:19,20. An altar was built to signify a new season before or immediately after life-altering (no pun intended) situations.

Whatever we worship has a spiritual altar in our life. (Exodus 20:3-6) We must make sure it is Jesus. If those heroes of the faith gave special attention to an altar (sacrifice and repentance) in a new season, it is wise to consider this same spiritual concept for ourselves. When Jesus became our sacrifice for sins, we no longer needed the actual physical altar for a priest to kill sacrifices for our wrongdoings. Now we have our own personal altars, whether it is a literal place you visit to pour out your heart in repentance before God or a time in your daily prayer that you focus on repentance. In Exodus 19, God wanted the Israelites to be prepared for His presence. It was a new chapter in their relationship with God, but they had a few days to prepare before this new level.

Exodus 19:10,11 "And the LORD said unto Moses, Go unto the people, and sanctify them to day and tomorrow, and let them wash their clothes, And be ready against the third day: for the LORD will come down in the sight of all the people upon mount Sinai."

This was repentance for the next level. Moses was about to receive laws and ordinances.

Before Jesus' ministry, his cousin John prepared the people with repentance and baptism. That was similar symbolically to the cleansing, purification, and also the sanctification process at Mt. Sinai. The Messiah (the law personified/the Word) was about to come on the scene. It was not a coincidence that John the Baptist's ministry created a foundational path of repentance and baptism. Both of these are monumental in preparing for deliverance, miracles, healings, and the infilling of the Holy Ghost. Repentance is crucial to remove the legality of sin and its effects so that deliverance and healing can occur.

Repentance is necessary for salvation: The following few pages consist of a quick recap of salvation if you are unfamiliar with it, as I once was. Repentance alone is not the only step in salvation, as we notice in Acts 18:25, 26; 19:1-6, and in the total content of Peter's first sermon on the day of Pentecost.

Acts 2:38 "Then Peter said unto them, Repent, and be baptized every one of you in the name of Jesus Christ for the remission *{859 aphesis – freedom, deliverance, forgiveness, release from bondage}*[1] of sins, and ye shall receive the gift of the Holy Ghost." (Repentance is the first step to the remission of sins.)

Repentance is the death of self-will, a discipline to "sacrifice" the old sinful flesh, desires, and motives. Baptism is symbolic of the washing and burial of that old self. (Acts 22:16; Romans 6:4) Receiving the Holy Spirit is resurrection – new life, being reborn - the breath of God living inside of you. (Romans 6:5; 8:9)

Repentance, water baptism in Jesus' Name, and receiving the infilling of the Holy Spirit with the evidence of speaking in other tongues are all necessary for salvation:

John 3:5, 8 "Jesus answered, Verily, verily, I say unto thee, Except a man be born of water and *of* the Spirit, he cannot enter into the kingdom of God." Verse 8 "The wind bloweth where it listeth, and thou hearest the sound thereof, but canst not tell whence it cometh, and whither it goeth: so is every one that is born of the Spirit."

Matthew 28:19 "Go ye therefore, and teach all nations, baptizing them in the name of the Father, and of the Son, and of the Holy Ghost:"

"Name" in that verse is singular, implying it is the same name for each, indicating one God. (Ephesians 4:5; James 2:19) You will also find nowhere in scripture where anyone is baptized in any other way except in Jesus' Name. (Acts 8:16; Galatians 3:27)

According to scripture in the New Testament, confession no longer must be before another man, such as a priest. It is important to apologize and own our mistakes to others if they were affected by the error, but Jesus is our High Priest now. (Hebrews 2:17; 3:1; 4:14-16; 5:6, 10; 6:20; 7:3, 11, 17, 21, 26-28; 8:1-4; 9:11) The concept of confession, as in Matthew 3:6, should help us to exchange silent, passive, generalized repentance for sincere, verbal, specific repentance. In our attempt to embrace Jesus as our High Priest, have we gradually forgotten the importance of verbally separating ourselves from sin? Could certain crucial aspects of the original meaning of repentance have been overlooked as time and traditions have occurred?

Let's look more closely at the translation definitions of <u>repentance</u>:

Repent:

<u>Shuv/Shub</u> – Hebrew OT 07725 – *to <u>turn</u> back or away, return, retreat, break, recall, convert, deliver, deny, pay, refresh, requite, repair, restore, reverse, rescue, withdraw, <u>reject</u>, refuse, revoke*[1] (II Chronicles 7:14)

Nacham – Hebrew OT 05162 – *"to be sorry, repent, regret, comfort, have compassion"*[1] (Job 42:6)

Strepho – Greek NT 4762 – *turn, change mind, converted*[1] (Matthew 18:3)

Metanoeo – Greek NT 3340 – *"to change one's mind, to repent. To heartily amend with abhorrence of one's past sins"*[1] (Matthew 3:2)

Here are just a few references for repentance:

2 Chronicles 7:14 "If my people, which are called by my name, shall humble themselves, and pray, and seek my face, and turn from their wicked ways; then will I hear from heaven, and will forgive their sin, and will heal their land."

Proverbs 28:13 "He that covereth his sins shall not prosper: but whoso confesseth and forsaketh {05800 *azab* – *to depart from, loose, forsake, set free*}[1] *them* shall have mercy."

(1 Kings 8:46-50; Isaiah 59:1, 2; Jeremiah 26:3, 13)

Psalms 32:5 "I acknowledged my sin unto thee, and mine iniquity have I not hid. I said, I will confess my transgressions unto the LORD; and thou forgavest the iniquity of my sin. Selah." (Also, notice Verses 6 and 7.)

In Psalms 51, David asks for his sins to be removed concerning his situation with Bathsheba at least 11 times, using 8 different terms. He even mentioned the possibility of his mother having committed the same sin in his confession. (Verses 3-5) David covered every base. He acknowledged and asked to be washed from his iniquities, to be cleansed from his sins, and for his transgressions to be blotted out. He also asked to be delivered from bloodguiltiness. David didn't stop there, though; he prayed restorative words of repair, rebuilding, and protection in Verses 8-15, 18. This is a complete example of true heartfelt repentance and faith that God is merciful. Once David saw his errors, he was quick to repent. I believe this attitude was one factor that made him a man after God's heart.

Psalms 139:23,24 "Search me, O God, and know my heart: try me, and know my thoughts: And see if *there be any* wicked way in me, and lead me in the way everlasting."

Matthew 4:17 "From that time Jesus began to preach, and to say, Repent: for the kingdom of heaven is at hand."

Mark 1:4,5 "John did baptize in the wilderness, and preach the baptism of repentance for the remission of sins. And there went out unto him all the land of Judaea, and they of Jerusalem, and were all baptized of him in the river of Jordan, confessing {1843 *exomologeo – acknowledge, profess, agree, confess, promise*}[1] their sins."

Luke 13:3 "I tell you, Nay: but, except ye repent, ye shall all likewise perish."

Luke 24:47 "And that repentance and remission of sins should be preached in his name among all nations, beginning at Jerusalem."

Acts 17:30 "And the times of this ignorance God winked at; but now commandeth all men every where to repent:" (the reason for repentance in Verse 31)

Romans 3:23 "For all have sinned, and come short {5302 *hystereo - late, inferior, lack, to fall behind*}[1] of the glory of God;"

Romans 6:23 "For the wages of sin *is* death; but the gift of God *is* eternal life through Jesus Christ our Lord."

2 Corinthians 7:10 "For godly sorrow worketh repentance to salvation not to be repented of: but the sorrow of the world worketh death."

Revelation 2:5 "Remember therefore from whence thou art fallen, and repent, and do the first works; or else I will come unto thee quickly, and will remove thy candlestick out of his place, except thou repent."

Revelation 2:21 "And I gave her space to repent of her fornication; and she repented not."

Revelation 2:21 indicates that there is possibly a space of mercy, as God allows before judgment. An example of that mercy on the nation of Israel, when they were in sin, is seen in Amos 3:7, "Surely the Lord GOD will do nothing, but he revealeth his secret unto his servants the prophets." (Also, Genesis 15:16) Of course, we do not know if there is always a grace period or warning before every judgment. Those few scriptures were meant for specific instances, but it does give us a glimpse into the abundant mercies of God.

Matthew 3:8 "Bring forth therefore fruits meet {514 *axios – worthy, due, deserving*}[1] for repentance:" (Also Luke 3:8)

John the Baptist indicated that the Pharisees and Sadducees were not sincere. Notice it again mentions works in the following verses:

Acts 26:20 "But shewed first unto them of Damascus, and at Jerusalem, and throughout all the coasts of Judaea, and *then* to the Gentiles, that they should repent and turn to God, and do works meet {514 *axios – worthy, due, deserving*}[1] for repentance."

James 2:20 "But wilt thou know, O vain man, that faith without works is dead?"

Revelation 3:2-5; 17-19; 16:15 - Repentance, watching, and being clothed (spiritually) in white raiment are instructed. 2 Corinthians 5:2-4, Matthew 22:11-14, and Jude 1:23 all speak about being adequately clothed. (Also 2 Peter 3:14)

The Lord said to me once during prayer that in the natural, our clothing can be altered to fit us, but in the spiritual realm, *we* are altered to fit our spiritual clothing. In the same way, we can accumulate layers of sin staining our spiritual clothing. Any attempt at clothing ourselves spiritually is useless (Isaiah 64:6.)

If it is possible to receive the Holy Ghost before baptism, as found in Acts 10:47, could it also be possible to receive the Holy Ghost without getting rid of every attachment of the enemy? The following scriptures contain various Greek words used in the idea of getting rid of sin, and as we will notice, they are all words written to Christians and/or churches.

Romans 13:12 "The night is far spent, the day is at hand: let us therefore cast off {659 *apotithemi – to put off or away*}[1] the works of darkness, and let us put on the armour of light."

2 Timothy 2:19 "Nevertheless the foundation of God standeth sure, having this seal, The Lord knoweth them that are his. And, Let every one that nameth the name of Christ depart {868 *aphistemi – remove, revolt, refrain, shun*}[1] from iniquity."

Titus 2:12 "Teaching us that, denying {720 *arneomai – reject, refuse, disavow, deny*}[1] ungodliness and worldly lusts, we should live soberly, righteously, and godly, in this present world;"

1 John 1:9 "If we confess {3670 *homologeo – acknowledge, covenant, declare, profess*}[1] our sins, he is faithful and just to forgive {863 *aphiemi – omit, abandon, send away, bid to depart*}[1] us *our* sins, and to cleanse {2511 *katharizo – purge, make clean*}[1] us from all unrighteousness."

Interesting fact: There is a Hebrew word – "modeh" - which incorporates the words admit and surrender with an idea of thankfulness or gratitude, creating a repentant gratefulness. There are several other Hebrew words used in praise and thanksgiving that also incorporate the word "confess." The total aspect of repentance could easily get lost in translation as some languages do not have words for the complexity of meanings.

Another word similar to "repent" and more closely related to the word "confess" is better expressed in its meaning through the Old Testament Hebrew word 07725 *shuv/shub*,[1] for its in-depth and verbal components. It is the term "renounced," found only once in the KJV, 2 Corinthians 4:2:

"But have renounced the hidden things of dishonesty, not walking in craftiness, nor handling the word of God deceitfully; but by manifestation of the truth commending ourselves to every man's conscience in the sight of God."

Renounced – Greek NT "550–*apeipomen*–*disown, renounce, to speak out, set forth, declare, forbid, give up,*"[1] (a combination of 575 –*apo* – *separation, departing, destroyed union or fellowship, off, away, cessation, completion, reversal, etc.*[1] and 2036 – *epo* – (connected to three other sources all meaning verbal communication) *to speak or command*[1]

In simple terms, renounce means to formally give up or reject. "Renounce" is a verbal revoking and is often used as a legal term. Jesus paid the ultimate price for our debt of sin that we could not pay, so the literal sacrifice is no longer necessary. Sacrificing had become legality or the work of the flesh when possibly the heart of man wasn't right or sincere. Many legal terms are used in scripture, indicating that the Lord is our Judge. (Acts 17:31; Romans 2:16; 14:10; 2 Timothy 4:1, 8; Hebrews 10:30; 12:23; James 4:11, 12; 5:9; 1 Peter 4:5, 6) John 12:48 says that the word that Jesus has spoken will judge. (Matthew 19:17-19; Romans 13:8-10)

Ezekiel 14:6, 7 is an example of thorough repentance and possibly renouncing, as well, because the same Hebrew word is used for "repent," "turn," and "turn away" in Verse 6.

It is essential for us to sincerely repent regularly and to be as specific as we can. We can do this by vocalizing errors privately and admitting them sincerely. It is imperative to *recognize* the problem to *avoid* that sin in the future.

True repentance takes humility, submission, honesty, sincerity, and forgiveness. I highly recommend specific renouncing when repenting, whether in the privacy of the home, in sign language for the deaf, or in a whisper for discretion. If you have repented to the Lord silently in your mind, that is fine, but renouncing cannot be done silently in the mind. I do not believe that all unclean spirits can read our minds in most cases, and if we give them orders of eviction in Jesus' Name, they must be able to receive the orders.

I remember repenting silently in my mind at the altar right before receiving the Holy Ghost. Looking back, I'm in awe of how loving and merciful the Lord was to accept my sincere repentance, even though I couldn't remember everything I had done wrong at that moment. I also wasn't aware of some things as being a sin. How could I repent for something I didn't even know was wrong? That fact alone should let us know that deliverance can continue past initial salvation. In my sincere state, I didn't care what I had to do or give up; I just wanted Jesus. Even though I had not been raised to attend church and, therefore, didn't understand many things, He stepped past everything I didn't understand to bring me to a greater place. And He still is!

The true essence of repentance incorporates renouncing, *not an added step for salvation*, but a more thorough repentance useful for *freedom*. It's similar to writing something negative, asking forgiveness, but never retracting or erasing the statement. In the English language, admitting my wrong is confessing – Being sorry, asking forgiveness, and turning to God is repenting – Verbalizing this and choosing to separate from that sin is renouncing. These are all aspects of true repentance.

We don't have to be professional at repenting, nor do we need to remember everything we've ever done wrong to receive the Holy Ghost. Once we have God's Spirit living inside us, with His help, we can step further into repentance to find even more freedom. I am living proof that a person can receive God's Spirit without understanding everything. Also, we do not need to get stuck in condemnation or a continuous cycle of feeling guilty and repenting of old sins. I will mention more about that later.

My husband preached a memorable message of repentance on a small island in Mexico years ago. I must brag on God for giving him a brilliant way to explain the process. The explanation was simple enough for every age and intellect. He explained that we are all like a cup full of contaminated liquid. There is no room left in a full vessel to fill with anything else, but when you empty the cup, it can be cleaned and refilled with good – the Holy Spirit. The people and visitors of that island responded with such sincere humility, and everyone that poured out themselves in exchange for God's Spirit was filled.

Sometimes we have closed off sections in our vessel that haven't yet been emptied or cleaned. I refer to this as the P.O.U.R. Effect – P.O.U.R. – Power Of Understanding Repentance. We have to P.O.U.R. if we want more of God.

CHAPTER 5
RENOVATION

Repentance leads to Renovation:

The words "refresh," "restore," and "repair" are also found in the Hebrew definition of repent. In each of the three words, action is required to bring about a renovation. Renovation should result from repentance: removing the old and making improvements. You can also use the phrase: "spiritual detox." I don't intend to exhaust the subject of repentance, but I want to point out some crucial factors that will create a foundation for a better understanding of deliverance.

Renovation:

Renew: Romans 12:2; 2 Corinthians 4:16; Ephesians 4:22-24; Colossians 3:8-10; Titus 3:5

If we want to advance in our relationship with God, a season of repentance leading to renewal is a wise next step. Something similar is mentioned in the Old Testament: "the year of release," also known as the Shmita – 08059 *shmittah* – *the seventh year of rest, reflection, and a release from debts.*[1] Israelite creditors were commanded to release their Israelite brethren from debts. It is a rest for the agricultural world of sowing and reaping, as seen in the Old Testament. (Exodus 23:10, 11; Leviticus 25:1-7, 20-22; Deuteronomy 15:1-18) It is beneficial to the poor and animals and allows the earth to be replenished. In fact, Israel was punished after failing to uphold this ordinance in 2 Chronicles 36:19-21. A spiritual season of reflection and release, like the Shmita year, is an excellent time to take inventory and ask God to remind us of things we should repent and release from our life. This release brings about changes and improves our spiritual environment, just like the renovation of a house.

Several times in scripture, we are compared to a house, tabernacle/tent, building, and also a temple: (Matthew 7:24-27; 12:29; Luke 11:24; 1 Corinthians 3:16; 6:19; 2 Corinthians 5:1, 2; Ephesians 2:22; 1 Peter 2:5). The idea that our "house," or spiritual man doesn't need work occasionally, is a deception.

Have you ever owned a house that didn't need to be cleaned, repaired, or renovated? Sometimes the walls need to be removed. Running into a spiritual wall has always required removing something inside me that did not belong. Sometimes storms come through, causing damage and exposing weaknesses. A new house may not require extensive work, but it does require regular cleaning. Homes have rooms, and I'm convinced God will clean and fill as many spaces as we allow Him access. It isn't fun to declutter and can be very costly to renovate. However, when it is over, you will most likely look back and wonder how you lived like that before the changes. (Ephesians 3:16-19)

Once, I asked my husband to patch a tiny rust spot in the tub of our older home, which we had lived in for just a few years. It started with harmless cleaning and ended in a complete remodel/renovation of the whole bathroom! On the surface, we only saw the tiny rust spot until he accidentally poked a hole in the tub while trying to fix the rust. That was when he discovered a small leak that had been happening for years! Trying to fix the leak, he uncovered black mold…lots of it! If you've ever ventured into repairs or have witnessed remodeling, you understand that one thing can frequently lead to another. The longer that problems remain hidden, the more damage there will be.

The issue: An *unknown* problem *cannot* be fixed. Many times, our spiritual renovation is the same way. We encounter an issue that uncovers another. Each layer reveals something else we didn't know existed or even a revelation of something we thought belonged to our original structure but doesn't. We hide things from ourselves. (Jeremiah 17:9, 10; Proverbs 21:2) And sometimes, we have filters that prevent us from really seeing that we have a problem. It is important for us to rightly divide the Word of Truth. (2 Timothy 2:15,16) We should always remember to search the scriptures and pray for the Lord to lead us in understanding.

The following passages show us the importance and power of God's Word. We should use His Word to test our words, thoughts, and revelations because every form of counsel must agree with the Bible.

Hebrews 4:12, 13 "For the word of God *is* quick, {2198 *zao – alive,*}[1] and powerful, {1756 *energes – active, effectual*}[1] and sharper than any twoedged sword, piercing even to the dividing asunder of soul and spirit, and of the joints and marrow, and *is* a discerner {2924 *kritikos – judge*}[1] of the thoughts and intents of the heart. Neither is there any creature that is not manifest in his sight: but all things *are* naked and opened unto the eyes of him with whom we have to do."

2 Timothy 3:16, 17 "All scripture *is* given by inspiration of God, and *is* profitable for doctrine, for reproof, for correction, for instruction in righteousness: That the man of God may be perfect, thoroughly furnished unto all good works."

Galatians 1:8 "But though we, or an angel from heaven, preach any other gospel unto you than that which we have preached unto you, let him be accursed."

1 John 4:1, 2 "Beloved, believe not every spirit, but try {1381 *dokimazo – discern, examine, test*}[1] the spirits whether they are of God: because many false prophets are gone out into the world. Hereby know ye the Spirit of God: Every spirit that confesseth that Jesus Christ is come in the flesh is of God:"
   (Notice in this scripture, we are instructed to try [or test] the spirits. Verse 2 tells us how, and in Verse 6, we discover there is both a spirit of *truth* and *error*.)

Proverbs 21:2 "Every way of a man *is* right in his own eyes: but the LORD pondereth the hearts."

Romans 12:2 "And be not conformed to this world: but be ye transformed by the renewing {342 *anakainosis – renovating*}[1] of your mind, that ye may prove {1381 *dokimazo – discern, examine, test*}[1] what *is* that good, and acceptable, and perfect, will of God."

These last words in Romans were letters to churches, so it applies to all Christians, new and aged.

How do we decide what is a part of our natural character (that we should prayerfully ask God to refine as well) or something that masks as our natural character? In prayer, we can ask for revelation in this matter. Do you remember a time that you did not have this personality trait? Is this a trait that you can't seem to control, no matter how much you've tried? If you've answered "yes" to either of these, there is no harm in repentance and then moving on to renouncing. Renouncing can cause manifestation. If you have ever sincerely repented for and renounced character flaws and then noticed a manifestation of some kind, chances are it is not a natural flaw but an attachment that can be removed. This does not remove our responsibility to choose the correct actions and behavior. Unfortunately, every flaw is not the result of a spirit. I say this because the removal of the spirit can produce instant results, which is much easier than a natural commitment to changing negative behavior.

"Manifestation" can be a scary word for those exposed to situations that may have been mishandled or for those exposed to the Hollywood version of the word. "Manifestation" in deliverance means *a symptom or noticeable sign of an attachment*. There are examples of this in scripture. (Mark 9:18, 20, 26; Luke 4:41; Acts 8:7) Growling, shrieking, screaming, falling out, gagging, foaming at the mouth, and strange movements are just a few more extreme examples of manifestations. There can also be subtle symptoms when attachments leave, such as simply coughing, sneezing, or just a feeling of release. Many are frightened by this idea, but a spirit manifests mostly to cause distraction and fear. Fear and distraction are its top two defense mechanisms because it wants to *remain.* Spirits can be attached to emotions and physical flesh inside our bodies, so just because a physical manifestation happens, that doesn't mean the person is "possessed" or owned by a demon. *If manifestation happens and then stops, this does not always guarantee the attachment has gone.* Often there will be a peaceful feeling of release felt among those participating or aiding in the deliverance when an attachment is truly gone. Also, sometimes an obvious manifestation does not happen at all. It is wise to revisit areas that have been dealt with to ensure everything is, in fact, gone. At times, a manifestation can also be bound. A very common manifestation I have noticed is a mournful cry that can sometimes be similar to stubborn child-like whining.

Lack of understanding and fear of the unknown have fueled the hesitance to discuss this topic, or possibly it has been addressed in the past, and a dark atmosphere resulted. If a presence of darkness is felt when discussing these things, it could be because someone in the room needs deliverance. Another reason for this feeling could be that the enemy doesn't want his tactics exposed. If our motives are right and we give Jesus all the glory for His power, there is no reason to fear discussing deliverance.

Also, there are common misconceptions about spirits going from one person to another during deliverance. Sometimes a manifestation in someone triggers a manifestation in another person. This does not mean the attachment was contagious. I do not have scripture for this theory, but I believe attachments are *assigned* by the enemy and require our permission through the sin associated with that spirit. I do not believe a spirit can attach to any random person just because that person is nearby or watching. Jesus performed deliverance in public many times.

It is healthy to take inventory of our inner man regularly. It is up to us to partner with God to ask for sensitivity and to discern if our flaws are spiritual or human imperfections that have been inherited or maybe resulted from our environment as learned behavior. As mentioned before, it is crucial to maintain a balance, especially for those engaging in spiritual warfare. Every sickness, syndrome, or disorder does not necessarily stem from a spirit or spiritual issue. Carnality or flesh cannot be cast out and will not necessarily respond to rebuke or anything of a spiritual nature. The flesh must be crucified through repentance, self-control, discipline, and temperance.

Our flesh needs discipline. We should care for the physical body/fleshly house God gave us. A proper diet, plenty of water, exercise, and adequate sleep go a LONG way toward being a good steward of the fleshly house. We can also be disciplined in our mind's diet and exercise through prayer, fasting, and devotion time. This is necessary if we want a thriving relationship with Him. If you do not have self-control in one area, you can ask Jesus to help you, but self-control and self-discipline alone will not remove evil spiritual attachments.

Visible dirt, a wound, or physical pain demands our attention. It's important to remember to tend to the inner man too. Internal injuries are the worst because we can't see what is happening. All internal injuries aren't physical, however. Just as a physical wound can become infected with contaminants, so can emotional or spiritual wounds become infected with contamination from the enemy. An injury is an opportune time for the adversary to slip impurities into our pain and remain without us realizing it.

I had a vision once of walking down a narrow hallway. It was narrow because both sides of the hallway were lined with hurt, pain, trouble, or things I couldn't process when they happened. The stuff had accumulated. So, as I grew spiritually, it was hard to move without bumping into everything. I had not been giving my troubles to the Lord. Instead, I had let them pile up, and while on my way to the next level, they were now obstacles.

In a study conducted at the University of Michigan, social psychologist Ethan Kross and several colleagues were able to see a similar response in the brain to both physical pain and social rejection. The researchers used fMRI scans on 40 individuals who had experienced break-ups compared to 500 previous responses of physical pain. They noticed the same regions of the brain were activated in both cases.² An article for Forbes in 2015 by Nicole F. Roberts also stated that Case Western Reserve University research showed an instant and significant drop in reasoning and IQ levels during rejection. When physical pain occurs, the brain responds with a natural painkilling opioid which is also released during an emotional hurt. Depending on certain personalities and how they process pain, responses vary among individuals. ³

This lets us know that inner pain is just as severe to our brain, so we shouldn't attempt to cover it ourselves or file it away in a "junk drawer" or mental-to-do list for later. We should take it to Jesus as soon as we get the opportunity and let Him care for our wounds as only He can. Emotional pain can become heavy. Carrying around unnecessary things will prevent us from going to higher places.

<u>Hebrews 12:1</u> "Wherefore seeing we also are compassed about with so great a cloud of witnesses, let us lay aside {659 *apotithemi – cast off, put off*}[1] every weight,{3591 *onkos - burden, encumbrance, hinderance*}[1] and the sin which doth so easily beset {2139 *euperistatos – surrounds, thwarts*}[1] *us*, and let us run with patience the race that is set before us,"

---

[2] *Study illuminates the 'pain' of social rejection.* Ann Arbor (03/25/11) Vice President for Communications Michigan News, University of Michigan.
https://www.news.umich.edu/study-illuminates-the-pain-of-social-rejection/
[3] *Rejection And Physical Pain Are The Same To Your Brain.* Nicole F. Roberts. (12/25/15, 06:00 am EST) Healthcare. Forbes.
https://www.forbes.com/sites/nicolefisher/2015/12/25/rejection-and-physical-pain-are-the-same-to-your-brain/?sh=72f59234f87f

(*Lay aside* – 659 *apotithemi*[1] – is a combination of two Greek words – 575 – *apo* – *separation, departing, destroyed union, off, away, cessation, reversal, etc.*[1] and 5087 *tithemi* – *to put down*.)[1]

Weight, in the previous verse, appears different than sin. In mountain biking, I know a few things about extra weight. If you attempt to reach a higher altitude, unnecessary weight eventually becomes a problem. The farther or higher you go, the heavier it gets. It is normal and healthy for God to reveal things or issues that need to be removed in a repentance/renovation season. We might not be able to ascend to the next level with the extra weight. Maybe it wasn't noticeable or heavy before, but because you are climbing, it is becoming a burden. If there is a weight we struggle with, Jesus is ready to help if we ask. Each new level has required something of me. If you want to go higher and deeper in God, it is essential to be willing to lay aside weight when God reveals it.

Do not ignore the convictions that God brings to your attention. However, it is <u>NEVER</u> wise to *permanently* lay something down without prayer. Picking something back up after promising to lay it down brings attention in the spirit realm – because it breaks a type of covenant. This does not reference standards for a specific time or place, temporarily doing without, or respecting others' convictions. But instead, I'm referring to a situation of feeling to permanently remove something from your life that is not commonly considered "sin" to get closer to God. He knows we are human and wants us to be careful in making vows. (Numbers 30:1-16; Deuteronomy 23:21-23; Ecclesiastes 5:4-6; James 5:12)

Sins bring us into agreement with our enemy. Romans 8:13 says, "…. if ye through the Spirit do mortify {2289 *thanatoo – destroy, liberate from bondage*}[1] the deeds {4234 *praxis – transaction, deal*}[1] of the body, ye shall live." Our sins can be transactions in the spirit realm. Following are a few verses and Biblical definitions for sin and similar terms:

Sin – Hebrew 02403 chattaah – *an offense, sin, guilt, uncleanness*;[1] Greek 266 hamartia n.– *no share in, err, wander, miss the mark, mistaken*[1] 264 hamartano v.[1]

Iniquity – Hebrew 05771 avon – *perversity, guilt*;[1] Greek 458 anomia – *illegality, wickedness, contempt, violate* [1]

Trespass – Hebrew 06588 pesha – *rebellion, revolt*;[1] Greek 264 hamartano – *err, miss the mark* [1]

Transgress – Hebrew 05674 abar - *cross over, overflow, provoke*;[1] Greek 3845 parabaino – *overstep, abandon* [1]

Romans 14:23 "…for whatsoever *is* not of faith is sin."

James 4:17 "Therefore to him that knoweth to do good, and doeth *it* not, to him it is sin."

James 2:10 "For whosoever shall keep the whole law, and yet offend in one *point*, he is guilty of all."

1 John 1:10 "If we say that we have not sinned, we make him a liar, and his word is not in us."

Matthew 19:17 "And he said unto him, Why callest thou me good? *there is* none good but one, *that is*, God: but if thou wilt enter into life, keep the commandments."

Instruction, commandments, laws, and covenants are given throughout scripture. These laws were given for our *protection*. In Matthew Chapters 5-7, Jesus repeated commandments and expounded on them. He was addressing the root of the problem. It is more than just rules; there is a *spiritual* aspect. Jesus stated that He came to fulfill the law, not destroy it. (Matthew 5:17-20) Most commandments were also repeated in Romans 13:9, 10.

Matthew 22:36-40 paraphrasing in my words – Jesus said to love the Lord thy God with all thy heart, soul, and mind, and then love thy neighbor as thyself – Verse 40 "On these two commandments hang all the law and the prophets."

1 John 2:1-6; 1 John 4:7, 8; 1 John 5:2, 3 (Paraphrased in my words: If we love God, we will keep His commandments, and God is love.)

1 Corinthians 13:4-8 describes the Characteristics of Agape Love:

1 John 4:18 "There is no fear in love; but perfect love casteth out fear: because fear hath torment. He that feareth is not made perfect in love."

Both sin and purpose make us a definite target of the enemy, not because God is waiting for us to fail, but because the enemy is. For example, look quickly at a group of mysterious verses from Exodus 4. At the beginning of the chapter, we have a dialogue between the Lord and Moses about returning to Egypt to free the Hebrew people. God gave instructions to Moses. As Moses was on his way to do what God had instructed, something unusual happened:

Exodus 4:24-26 "And it came to pass by the way in the inn, that the LORD met him, and sought to kill him. Then Zipporah took a sharp stone, and cut off the foreskin of her son, and cast *it* at his feet, and said, Surely a bloody husband *art* thou to me. So, he let him go: then she said, A bloody husband *thou art*, because of the circumcision."

That is all that is mentioned on the subject. There is much speculation and reading between the lines because the brief context is vague. According to some Bible scholars, there is a Midianite tradition that a Midianite son would be circumcised around the time of his wedding. There was possibly a compromise and understanding between Moses and his Midianite wife. It seems, though, in the mindset of spiritual warfare, that whenever God spoke to Moses and gave him the plan and authority, Moses came again on the enemy's radar. The enemy's radar looks for sin. (Revelation 12:10 refers to the devil as "...the accuser of our brethren...which accused them before our God day and night.")

Previously in Genesis 17:1-14, God had made a covenant with Abraham. He not only promised to be his God but also promised the land his seed would one day possess. Circumcision was commanded as a sign of the covenant to Abraham concerning this:

Genesis 17:14 "And the uncircumcised man child whose flesh of his foreskin is not circumcised, that soul shall be cut off from his people; he hath broken my covenant."

Did the accuser of the brethren appear before God, remind God of this law concerning circumcision, and point out that one of Moses' sons was not yet circumcised? If this was the case, this was a *legal* opportunity for judgment, especially since Moses was making a crucial step toward the promised land.

After Jesus died for our sins, the matter of circumcision was of great controversy among the new Gentile and Jewish believers. In the New Testament, Paul mentioned it often as a spiritual type and shadow (1 Corinthians 7:18; Colossians 2:11) and indicated it was no longer commanded under the new law of liberty. The fact that the previous strict and significant law was no longer necessary was possibly tough to receive.

Commandments and laws were created for our *protection*. Sin ultimately separates, damages our hedge/covering, and compromises our relationship with Jesus. The result is a trickle effect for other relationships to become compromised. The end results, aided by pride, are then bitterness and unforgiveness.

God purchased us with His Blood, not because we are good enough, but because He is. If we follow traditions and guidelines without a relationship, although the discipline is commendable, we miss the point. The Lord wants to protect us from becoming entangled by sin, both physically and spiritually. Beware of modern-day pharisaical *legalism*. That is a dangerous and deceptive self-righteous *spirit* with the following symptoms: a tendency toward judgment, being critical, resentful, and bitter. Those who deal with this *spirit* will focus mostly on law, separating themselves from those they consider to be in sin because of differences. True love does not reject those who are different; it embraces them. How will people feel drawn to the love of Jesus if we respond with judgment and rejection? Being kind and loving someone doesn't mean you approve if they are in sin. Pharisaical legalism is a very deceptive spirit because it twists what is *right*, making the motives wrong and destructive. They justify their righteousness through their works. The Pharisees held strongly to law and traditions while overlooking purpose, grace, mercy, and love. (Matthew 12:1-8; 23:23-28) We must obey God's laws, but those laws were created to help us toward unity and peace with mercy, faith, and love as the true goal.

CHAPTER 6
BRIERS AND THORNS

In prayer about the subject of deliverance, God interrupted and instructed me to go to a specific place behind my house, where He would continue speaking with me. I obeyed and ventured to where He told me to go. It was a few minutes before I heard the Lord whisper, "Look around. What do you see?"

I answered in my mind, 'The woods, but they're difficult to see with these ugly dead briers hanging in my way.'

"Yes, but what else do you notice?" He asked.

Nothing was coming to me.

"Look closely at those briers in your way." He had to give me a hint. "Didn't you cut those vines last year?"

'Oh yeah!' I thought, and suddenly, I got it. I looked around, and some of the greenbrier vines I had cut down to the ground had grown back and were thriving as if winter had never happened. Because the season was still at the beginning of spring, I could see them perfectly in contrast to the dead ones. *Sometimes we can only see things in certain seasons.* Maybe I was in this very season figuratively so that God could reveal the flaws He wanted to remove and the ugly dead things still clinging to me that I had cut off long ago.

Sometimes our pain and brokenness push us to a place where we are desperate enough to finally see what God has wanted to remove from us for a long time. I had diligently chopped off every noticeable brier at its base to the ground. Completely uprooting them is the only way to prevent their overgrowth. However, I didn't remove all of the clinging old vines for apparent reasons, and there they remained, hanging from trees and bushes, snagging, and piercing anyone who got too close. Even though I had cut off their life supply, they would be attached until they were removed, and I had to recognize them before they could be removed. If I ever embraced them again, though, they would hurt me.

We all go through seasons in our journey. Sometimes our paths become entangled over time. Relationships can become messy, with unforgiveness sprouting from misunderstandings. Unforgiveness is a sinful fruit. Its seeds lodge just under the surface, creating a root of bitterness that grows deeper over time. The root of bitterness then attaches and defiles us. (Hebrews 12:14, 15)

On a side note, have you ever encountered a thorn or splinter breaking off into your flesh? If it is deep enough to prevent immediate removal, it is uncomfortable at first, but after a while of leaving it, you hardly notice it is there. If it is very deep, your flesh can grow over the entrance, but eventually, most small foreign objects like that will work their way to the surface and then are easily removed. That is the way our flaws can be over time. You first ignore the discomfort and soon forget about it, but that doesn't mean it is gone. One day it will resurface, and until then, it is a foreign matter that doesn't belong, connected but working its way out of the flesh.

Galatians 5:1 "Stand fast therefore in the liberty wherewith Christ hath made us free, and be not entangled again with the yoke of bondage."

As this scripture appears to be referring to the Jewish law and circumcision, it can also be an important scripture about the fact that believers can be entangled *again*, and the description of the "yoke of bondage" clarifies the spiritual aspect of our old man. In the following verse, we will see another aspect where the concept of an unclean spirit seems closely related to a dead brier or vine.

Matthew 12:43-45 "When the unclean {169 *akathartos – impure, foul, demonic*}[1] spirit is gone out of a man, he walketh through dry places, seeking rest, and findeth none. Then he saith, I will return into my house from whence I came out; and when he is come, he findeth *it* empty, swept, and garnished. Then goeth he, and taketh with himself seven other spirits more wicked than himself, and they enter in and dwell there: and the last *state* of that man is worse than the first. Even so shall it be also unto this wicked generation."

It is important to encourage anyone who has experienced freedom to follow up by filling every empty spot with the Holy Ghost. However, this verse indicates that the unclean spirit still had legal rights to that man because it refers to the man as "my house." It doesn't mention the unclean spirit being "cast out" 1544 *ekballo – drive or cast out,*[1] but instead, 1831 *exerchomai – go out of*.)[1]

The presumed derivative for 169 *akathartos*[1] in Matthew 12:43 is 2508 *kathairo* meaning *to prune vines or purge*.[1] Thorns are also often mentioned in connection with curses in the Bible. (Genesis 3:18)

In Matthew 12:44, the Greek word for "house" – 3624 *oikos* also means *family*,[1] and the word "last" – 2078 *eschatos* in Verse 45 also relates to a sense of *contiguity*.[1] I thought it odd that Jesus would go from talking about that generation's judgment to throwing a quick lesson on spiritual warfare for the Pharisees who had badmouthed his ministry. The key could be in the word *generation*. He said *generation* five times in Matthew 12. Was He warning them that the following generations could suffer from the Pharisees' scrutiny, their spiritual blindness, and lack of faith? Could He have been hinting that the Pharisees were becoming more bound with each generation or even the possibility of a generational curse?

The Pharisees' scrutiny sounds much like today's rigid religious societies. The criticism of the deliverance ministry is nothing new. Our adversary will use every tactic he can because freedom weakens his kingdom. In Verses 22-26, the Pharisees accused Jesus of casting devils out by Beelzebub. Jesus indicated that kingdoms were weakened by the removal of devils from people in those territories and then warned against blasphemy. We should be extremely careful in our discernments and judgments of what we label as being of the devil or of the Holy Ghost.

As I stated before, sin can create an opening in the spiritual hedge, covering, or door (of which we are clothed with the metaphorical "house.") This provides a legal right for the enemy. (Door- Genesis 4:7; James 5:9) If you have been acquainted with intercessory prayer, you have most likely heard the terms "hedge" and "gap."

Hedge - (Surrounds and provides protection.)
Job 1:10 – 07753 <u>suwk</u> – *to entwine, fence, protection*[1]
Ecclesiastes 10:8 – "01447 <u>gader</u> – *fence, wall*"[1]
Isaiah 5:5 – "04881 <u>msuwkah</u> – *hedge*"[1]
Ezekiel 13:5; 22:30 also contains both *gaps* – "*06556* <u>*perets*</u> *- a break, breach, gap, breaking forth, broken wall, bursting forth*"[1] and *hedge -* 01447 <u>gader</u> [1]

On one occasion, years ago, I remember a night when my husband was working out of town, and I awoke in the middle of the night very aware there was an evil spirit in the room. I immediately began praying and became frustrated when I couldn't get the evil presence to leave. God spoke to me, letting me know that the spirit was there because it was attracted to the sin I had hidden in my heart. God told me I could pray all night, and it would not leave until I truly repented for what was in my heart and mind concerning a specific individual. I had not physically sinned toward that person in my actions. Although I had heard many sermons on sin and other obvious sources of demonic activity, I had not heard that evil spirits had legal rights to attack or stay because of sin. God revealed critical information that sin, hidden or open, eventually attracts the demonic like a magnet to metal and has the right to stay until that sin is removed. It's as if the longer the sin remains, the more likely it provides a dwelling place or stronghold for the enemy, who will invite more guests.

If the enemy can get us divided on technicalities, he has distracted us from the primary goal, which is freedom. The enemy uses fear and tradition, which cultivate resistance to the idea that we could be bound because we are saved. We don't have to be deeply involved in sin to have an attachment. If you are resistant to the possibility of an attachment, ask yourself why you are immune to this. If the enemy can attack our minds by giving us unclean or negative thoughts, why couldn't he attack us in other ways? Those thoughts don't force us to sin unless we leave them unchecked and let them move in. Then he has evidence against us.

<u>How do we engage in warfare? It involves seven key factors - faith, submission, the Word, praise, worship, prayer, and fasting. Anyone full of the Holy Spirit can help with deliverance. Still, it is better to be spiritually prepared</u>: cleansed through repentance (and renouncing,) having received baptism in Jesus' Name, filled with the Holy Spirit, clothed with the whole armor of God (which is mentioned in more detail later) and continuing as both sin and weight free. (1 John 2:16) None of us can be perfect on our own, and human perfection is not a requirement when engaging in spiritual warfare. However, those who regularly engage in warfare

should do their best to be consistent in prayer, reading and studying the Bible, fasting if possible, faithfulness and submission to authority and church, being a good steward, and reaching others. This is spiritual conditioning for a soldier going into a spiritual battle. Evil spirits love to expose weaknesses and sin, but if the blood of Jesus covers your sin, there is no reason to fear.

If you cannot be submitted to a man of God, you have no business in warfare or deliverance. There are ranks of authority in the spirit realm and on Earth. I am not implying that we should submit to dictators who abuse authority. However, submission to a true man of God will bring protection and covering, transference of anointing, and blessing through humility and obedience. We all need counsel and correction at times. That is the pruning that produces healthy growth. And remember, anointed leaders are still living in the flesh, so we are to extend grace when they make mistakes and pray for them.

In addition to the "briers" concept, briers and thorns were not mentioned positively in the Bible. In Matthew 13:7, 22, they are referred to as the cares of this world. Luke 6:44 and Hebrews 6:8 both use them in reference to men being known by their fruit in a bad sense. In 2 Corinthians 12:7, Paul's "thorn in the flesh" was known as the "messenger of Satan." My favorite scripture with thorns is Hosea 2:6 because, in the next verse, the hedge of thorns was the preeminence to a return – the same Hebrew word often used for "repentance."

Numbers 33:51-56 are God's instructions for the children of Israel to drive out the trespassers from the promised land. Driving out those in bondage to the abominations and sins of that time is seen all throughout Old Testament history. The Old Testament was full of *literal* bondage and captivity. These captivities are types and shadows of spiritual bondage. In Numbers 33:55, the opposition that was not driven out of the promised land was compared to *thorns*, and this wording is also used in Joshua 23. We see a similar situation in 2 Chronicles 33:9-13. Again, the word "thorns" is seen when describing where the king of Assyria captured Manasseh. A parallel was happening. The spiritual condition of Israel was seen in their literal captivity. The New Testament speaks of freedom from *spiritual* bondage and captivity. The sophisticated mindset of the religious leaders of that time focused on literal captivity and what they could see. Jesus was doing a new thing, trying to set them spiritually free. It did not fit into their idea of a classy or sophisticated Messiah.

In Hebrews 6:1, 2, the writer of Hebrews encouraged the Hebrew people to mature spiritually. The author didn't appear to lessen the importance of the foundational things necessarily but seemed frustrated with their spiritual immaturity. (Hebrews 5:12-14)

Here's where it gets tricky. Hebrews 6:4-6 used to be my least favorite scriptures because I couldn't make sense of them. I have heard several ideas and interpretations. Religious culture most likely struggled with transitioning away from strict laws, ceremonies, and traditions. Even though the writer mentions the concept of putting Jesus to open shame by crucifying Him again in Verse 6, I'm not convinced that his concern was about repetitious religious traditions.

While writing this, the Lord repeatedly prompted me to read Verses 4-8. I was trying to understand why two fields were mentioned after Verse 6. Also, why would the writer chasten them about not being spiritually mature, then mention the fallen state of a Christian who had once walked in the spirit realm? Why would he say it was impossible for the one who had fallen away to be renewed again by repentance? We know from the story of the prodigal son in Luke 15:11-32 and several other scriptures that have already been mentioned that God has abundant mercy. I was initially taught that Hebrews 6:4-6 meant that those who have walked away from God did not have the guarantee of a second chance. I studied many other views considering the history and context. It was also possible that the early Hebrew church had struggled with discernment between those sincere in their conversions and those with sinister motives. That would've been easier to hide in the previous days when traditions took preeminence.

However, I reread those verses regarding what can spiritually happen to backsliders, and suddenly it clicked. It is impossible, *just* through repentance, to make them born again since they have already been reborn once. They must be delivered. They most likely allowed things to creep in to initiate the falling away process. Those things have to be removed. Repentance is a good start, but asking for forgiveness and not addressing the problem might prove ineffective in the long term. It confirms this idea in Hebrews 6:8, "But that which beareth thorns and briers *is* rejected, and *is* nigh unto cursing; whose end *is* to be burned." This verse must refer to the fruit of those who fall away. Interestingly, one of the roots of the Greek word 5146 *tribolos*,[1] used for "briers," has its main root 956 *belos*[1] from 906 *ballo*,[1] the familiar root word used most for casting out spirits. The word "beareth" – 1627 *ekphero* in Greek ultimately means *to carry*.[1] In other words, those who have fallen away are possibly carrying things that need to be removed and therefore need deliverance, not *just* repentance. If they encounter issues returning to the Lord, a thorough repentance sparking deliverance is key. This does NOT mean all who have fallen away need a dramatic Hollywood-style exorcism. Many times, deliverance is just a feeling of release and peace. The attachment or attachments that initiated the backsliding and whatever else was allowed access afterward, most likely need to be addressed and told to leave.

The writer of Hebrews was letting the Hebrew believers know that they needed to mature in the spirit realm. They were obviously knowledgeable about the foundation and principles of salvation but were handicapped by their lack of discernment and going deeper.

Two years ago, I had been foraging in my herb garden when I mistakenly grabbed a volunteer *brier*! On a day I wasn't watching, seeds had been planted, possibly from the flight of a bird. Over a short time, while camouflaged, the seeds grew. I was amazed at how much the brier resembled the other plants in its proximity, but I was careful to remove the brier immediately. I continued checking the area to find it trying to come back a few more times. Multiple seeds must have fallen there. Finally, I was able to get every root. If left unchecked, a brier will grow and thrive wherever it can.

The enemy always seems to have a counterfeit for what God does. Jesus is the true vine. (John 15:1-5) Our adversary is like a brier. (Matthew 13:7; Hebrews 6:8)

I know you are just hoping for more scripture references for thorns and briers. Well, here they are:

Numbers 33:55; Joshua 23:13; Judges 2:3; Proverbs 15:19; 22:5; Isaiah 7:23, 24; 10:17; 34:13; Jeremiah 4:3; 12:13; Ezekiel 2:6; 28:24; Hosea10:8

CHAPTER 7
THE WHO

This chapter is not about the '60s rock band; it is about the questions: <u>Who needs deliverance</u>? And <u>Who can participate in deliverance</u>?

If you are a Spirit-filled Christian, you are NOT exempt from the possibility of having an attachment. Neither are you exempt from the ability to cast out attachments. Having the Holy Spirit inside you does not yet free you from living in the flesh, where many attachments are. Genesis 3:15-19 lets us know that because they disobeyed God's words in the garden and sinned by partaking of the forbidden fruit, most curses were upon their flesh.

The following is a list of items or actions that are the most common avenues for evil spiritual attachments or attacks. If you or your family have ever been involved in any of these, even though it was done in ignorance, intended for harmless entertainment, or if you were a victim of trauma at no fault of your own, there could still be a legal attachment, especially if it has not been addressed and ordered to depart.

Idolatry: any type of worship other than that of Jesus, any covenant or contract connected with idols, pagan activities, religious legalism (Exodus 20:3-6, 17)

Witchcraft/ Occult Involvement: palm reading, tarot cards, ghost hunting, séances, occult items, fortunes, spells, magic, incantations, chants, automatic writing, telekinesis, astral projection, books on any of these subjects, blood oaths, charms-herbs-crystals, Halloween items, pentagrams, divination, Inappropriate entertainment, horoscopes, yoga, meditation, transcendental meditation, dream catchers, occult-themed videos, horror movies, games, and apps; explicit and inappropriate music and books; jewelry, apparel, décor, or items with occultic symbols/writing, any form of hypnosis, mind control, or any attempt to open the third eye (Deuteronomy 18:9-15; Acts 19:19)

Addictions: (especially drug use resulting in an altered state of mind, hallucinations, and memory loss)

Trauma: (trauma where emotions are altered, resulting in shock, prolonged emotional numbness or extended grief, extreme fear, anxiety, self-harm, or a personality change) violence, rape, molestation, etc.

Sexual Perversion: pornography, promiscuity, incest, and any sexual activity outside of Biblical marriage, including masturbation, and lust (Romans 1:27-32; Galatians 5:19-21; Revelation 21:8)

Unforgiveness: grudges, bitterness (Matthew 6:14, 15)

Illegal Activities: stealing, lying, murder, abortion, rebellion (Exodus 20:12-16)

Any Prolonged Sin: not taking thoughts captive, gossiping, speaking harmful words against people - especially speaking against those in authority and ministry. (Matthew 12:34-37; Philippians 4:8)

You are not alone if you have ever been a victim of or participated in any of these. I am not implying you definitely have an evil spirit if you have engaged in many of these, for instance, if you have thought a wrong thought. There is no way to know how much each person can sin before an attachment has an open door. This list was made from research and personal experiences with deliverances and is not intended to promote fear or legalism. It is just a reference guide to help pinpoint a possible doorway. God didn't create laws to see us fail and punish us. He is all merciful and wants our protection and prosperity. The enemy is the one who wants our demise. If you are a victim of trauma, visit that area in prayer. Check if that became an open door for fear, unforgiveness, or negative emotions. Trauma happens to almost everyone eventually. That is not a sin and often not our fault at all. Allowing sin to dwell in our minds or hearts during this time of weakness is the avenue the enemy tries to use.

This list might be controversial. You will not find each item listed specifically in the Bible, such as astral projection, for example, but be sure the questionable items were added for a reason. I could have benefitted from a list like this years ago.

Generational Curses:

Once again, every *attack* doesn't necessarily come from our own sin or even from sin at all. Notice Jesus' disciples asked, "Who did sin, this man, or his parents, that he was born blind?" Jesus didn't correct them after He answered, confirming the possibility that the sins of our ancestors can affect us. In John 9:1-3, a reason for the man's trial of blindness was for God's works to be made manifest.

There are many examples in the Old Testament where generations were reaping what their forefathers had sown. (Exodus 20:5; 34:7; Deuteronomy 5:9; 24:16; and Jeremiah 31:29-34) There is a similar principle called the law of the harvest mentioned in Galatians 6:7-9.

2 Samuel 21:1-14 speaks of a famine that occurred for three years. King David inquired of the LORD, and the LORD told him it was because Saul and his house slew the Gibeonites. Neither King David nor his kingdom was eternally responsible for what Saul did. However, they had truly suffered the consequences on Earth. The previous king had made decisions that caused suffering. Does this sound familiar? Today, generations will reap economic and other important decisions that previous political administrations have made. We didn't make those decisions, but they will still affect us. We are not spiritually responsible, judged, nor sentenced to death for the sins of our bloodline, but we may be affected either by association or directly in the flesh. At the same time, it is important to remember not to blame every issue we have on those who have lived before us. Repenting for the sins of our ancestors not only prevents certain cultures from idolizing them but also helps us to take responsibility and be accountable before God.

Asking Him to remove that stain from our bloodline helps prevent us from making the same mistakes.

If this idea is controversial, ask yourself: Do you believe in receiving blessings but do not believe in curses? Why did Paul feel it necessary to mention in Romans 12:14, "Bless them which persecute you: bless, and curse not." If curses no longer exist, why are they mentioned? (1 Corinthians 16:22; James 3:9-18; 2 Peter 2:14; Revelation 22:3;)

Research has already discovered some interesting findings and is ongoing concerning epigenetics. New York City's Icahn School of Medicine at Mount Sinai conducted a study in 2015. The Director of the Traumatic Stress Studies Division, Dr. Rachel Yehuda, found epigenetic changes to a gene that was linked to cortisol levels of the children of 40 Holocaust survivors. Cortisol functions as an important stress hormone. This genetic factor may affect the offspring's ability to deal with stress. Low cortisol levels in infants born to mothers who were pregnant during 9/11 and a specific genetic mark on children born during the Dutch famine just after WWII indicate that genes can be affected by the previous generation.[4] And so it seems that science confirms spiritual law.

Because of the time it takes to observe each human generation, various studies have been conducted on mice. One discovery was

---

[4] *Can Trauma Be Passed Down From One Generation to the Next?* How Extreme Situations Have Impacted Offspring. Paragraphs 1-4. Karina Margit Erdelyi. (08/31/22) Medical Reviewer: Juli Fraga, PsyD.
https://www.psycom.net/trauma/epigenetics-trauma

in the offspring of mice carrying a genetic imprint from an association of a scent connected with pain experienced by the parents, even though the baby mice had not yet experienced the pain themselves.[5] This is an exciting discovery, although some are still skeptical, considering the influence of the environment or learned behavior. Whether it is a change in how the DNA is read or repeated behavior from environmental factors, it does not remove the idea that each generation can affect the next, but that doesn't have to be the end of the story. God specializes in removing flaws.

Suppose you can spot a pattern of negative issues or personality traits that have reoccurred from one generation to the next in your bloodline or family, such as diseases, addictions, personality traits, financial hardships, fears, relationship issues, prejudices, etc. – any of those could be resulting from generational or bloodline curses. The medical field has even noticed that genetics can play a role in tendencies for specific illnesses. If we are aware of our biological family, I'm sure most of us have patterns we can recognize after multiple generations. Bloodline curses are extremely common.

Ezekiel 18:20-24. The Lord spoke through Ezekiel that He preferred mercy and no longer wanted the son to bear the iniquity of his father or the father to bear his son's iniquity. In Israel's history, sometimes whole families faced death because of the sin of the leader of the house, as in the case of Korah in Numbers 16:31-33. Entire families could also be spared, as in the beautiful story of

---

[5] *Fearful Memories Haunt Mouse Descendants.* Callaway, E. Nature (12/01/13) https://doi.org/10.1038/nature.2013.14272

Rahab in Joshua 6:25. Ezekiel 18 lets us know that we are not responsible for each other's sins in a judgment fashion.

In Nehemiah 9:1-3, the Israelites, in humility, stood and confessed their sins and the sins and iniquities of their fathers. They possibly spent two hours and 45 minutes reading the Word and another two hours and 45 minutes confessing and worshipping. Nehemiah historically occurred after Ezekiel. If Ezekiel 18 had been referencing an end to generational curses, it is unlikely Israel would have spent time confessing the iniquities of their fathers. They knew the correct foundation for protection was thorough repentance.

Galatians 3:13 says that Jesus became a curse for us, and 2 Corinthians 5:21 says that Jesus was made to be sin for us. Sin didn't cease to exist because of this, but we have power over it through Jesus. Jesus is now our Father, and we have a new bloodline spiritually, but we are still living on earth in corruptible flesh and have not yet "put on incorruption."

Whatever knowledge we lack about our ancestors should not prevent us from repenting for them. I allow the Lord to lead me in prayer because He is completely supernatural – and knows everything about everyone. In my experience, some evil/unclean spirits aren't discovered until after bloodline curses have been broken. Asking the Lord for discernment is extremely helpful during these types of deliverances. It is common for God to give a name of a pagan god or goddess to renounce in which a manifestation results.

Often if the names are researched afterward, you can see a connection or a way it was in the bloodline. The following story is an example of a Holy Ghost-filled person (the name is changed) affected by a bloodline curse:

Once, Tom had a very unusual experience when God impressed him to repent for his forefather's involvement in a specific war. Although his forefather had not volunteered for that war, Tom felt God wanted him to focus more on addressing the government's decisions concerning that war in prayer. When he began to pray at first, he was praying out of obedience to what the Lord was telling him to do. When Tom, as a citizen under the authority of that government, repented of the government's decisions, involvement, and participation, and then repented and renounced his family member's participation in that war, he suddenly had a brief battlefield flashback. He felt physically as if he had grabbed onto an electric fence. The shock and sadness were so extreme that Tom couldn't help but cry out in prayer! Amazingly, he noted, it wasn't a long vision or prayer, but Tom knew he had broken something transferred through the bloodline. When Tom told another believing member of his family, she too tried this prayer, and possibly because of her closer generational involvement with the soldier, she had a lengthier, more vivid flashback. She felt much more intensity than Tom had. Tom had broken a curse connected with PTSD, and even though he didn't struggle with it, his child did. He noticed a change in the child's behavior after that.

If they had been carrying this as Holy Ghost-filled believers for years, could others carry baggage from war or associated trauma? This doesn't mean that war is wrong, as there were several wars already mentioned to bring about peace and freedom from the Old Testament times. If war was used with dark underlying purposes of corruption, however, it could be a snare.

The power of the blood of Jesus is the best solution for believers and unbelievers dealing with PTSD. I have not been in physical battles and have complete gratitude and respect for all soldiers who bravely and honorably fight for their country. I pray for all dealing with trauma to become aware of deliverance through Jesus' Name.

Who needs deliverance? NO ONE IS EXEMPT from the possibility of spiritual attachments. Our flesh is not immune to sin. If sin can be in our hearts or minds, so can an attachment. How can a spirit of infirmity or sickness attack our body while we are also filled with the Holy Ghost? To be attached, it doesn't have to be living inside our spirit. We have emotions and internal body parts inside our fleshly bodies as well.

Children can also have spiritual attachments. (Mark 9:21) Believing parents or guardians have authority over their children, especially if they are young and have not yet developed an understanding concerning repentance. The enemy targets children. It is less noticeable if he can get them while they are young and possibly create more of a stronghold. As Spirit-filled parents, we must remain alert and aware of all forms of entertainment, device apps, games, or toys that could be open doors for children.

Also, be aware of items you may have that could carry curses. Joshua 6:17, 18 tells us that some places and objects can be cursed. It is thought that Jericho was involved in moon worship. The city was cursed, and the Israelites were instructed not to take any cursed items for themselves. Idols and occult items are commonly cursed, which means certain spirits and purposes have been assigned to them.

Who can participate in deliverance? Any believer in Jesus can do this. However, demons can manifest and speak through the person, targeting the people assisting. Evil spirits can also plant poisonous seeds of discord because they may not always tell the truth. If commanded to tell the truth, especially with stubborn demons, information on how they came to be attached can be helpful. It is wise to refrain, however, if the communication is not beneficial for freedom or future prevention but is causing distraction, discouragement, confusion, or division. Jesus did, on occasion, question a spirit when it didn't leave right away. (Mark 5:9) It appears that when Jesus silenced an evil spirit, He did so to prevent His identity from being exposed before His time. (Mark 1:24, 25, 34; 3:11, 12) Always remember that we are not the ones doing anything. The power and authority of the Name of Jesus, His Blood, and His Word have the power to make them leave.

If you are helping with deliverance, it is better to enter the session having already experienced deliverance yourself and with a clear conscious. It is important to know that one deliverance doesn't mean you are entirely free. It took several sessions for me in self-deliverance. I still periodically check myself, especially if I react badly to a situation or have recurrent dreams indicating hidden sin. Let's face it; we get a bath or shower regularly. Why wouldn't we be proactive in checking and cleansing our spiritual man? Even if you disagree with generational curses, it does no harm to repent and renounce them. You might be surprised by what happens.

None of us are above possible corruption. (2 Corinthians 7:1) Spiritual warfare and deliverance are not *salvation* issues. They are *freedom* issues. God's Spirit can dwell inside of us, and we can still have a bad day or experience problems. God doesn't abandon us each time we sin. He is not afraid of sin. How many times have we been in sin and God has spoken to us or convicted us? His Spirit gives us *power* over sin but doesn't necessarily *prevent* it if we choose to sin.

CHAPTER 8
DOORWAYS

Doorways:

Some scriptures indicate specific points of access for the spirit realm. The following scriptures are focused on these as openings that allow the enemy legal rights.

Matthew 5:28, 29; 6:22, 23: the <u>eye</u> is a doorway.

Matthew 15:18; James 3:6: the <u>tongue</u> is another type of doorway

<u>Romans 10:17</u> "So then faith *cometh* by hearing, and hearing by the word of God." If faith can come by hearing, what counterfeit for faith does the enemy have that could also enter through our <u>ears</u>?

Matthew 15:19; Philippians 4:8: Indicating that our <u>mind</u> and <u>heart</u> are doorways.

1 Thessalonians 4:3, Ephesians 5:3, and 1 Corinthians 6:18- 20 all indicate that fornication and like-sins are defiling or sinning against/toward the <u>body</u>: another doorway.

At the same time, you can turn most of these access points around for good to fight spiritual warfare from an offensive angle. Sometimes if I'm not careful, I live in a defensive mindset regarding spiritual warfare. One day God told me, "You are not defense; you are offense." It stunned me at first, but "defense" was the way

I tended to think. I have worked to change my thinking from fear and avoidance of attack–defense; to facing the enemy the way God intended through His power and wisdom – offense.

Idolatry was and remains a serious foot in the door for the enemy. This is what God told me: When we join ourselves and connect in agreement with an idol, we are uniting ourselves to a demon. Idolatry and adultery were often synonymous in the Old Testament. When Israel began worshipping other gods, it was often as if they had committed adultery against God and chosen another. (These gods were demons. The word used for "devil" in the New Testament references "gods" and "goddesses" in its root definition.) Notice the references and similarity between adultery and idolatry in Jeremiah 3 and Ezekiel 16. I firmly believe that the Lord created the relationship of husband and wife to mirror an example for the Lord and His bride. If we understand the dynamics of a healthy marriage relationship, we will better understand what our relationship with Him should resemble.

In 2 Kings 18:4, Hezekiah had to destroy the brazen serpent Moses had made in Numbers 21:8 because it had become an idol. The very thing God used one time was not necessarily how He did a miracle the next time. That is why we must be sensitive to hearing the Lord's words in each new situation. We need to know the God of the miracle. The same could be said for anything we use superstitiously. Whatever we put faith in and choose over God can become our idol and thus joins us to something else.

In Genesis 15:6, Abraham was considered righteous because he believed God. In Verse 18, God made a covenant with him. In what many call the "Hall of Faith," Abraham is mentioned in Hebrews 11:8-19. Abraham's faith led to a covenant. A sobering thought: his faith in God's Word entered him into an agreement or covenant with God. If we have fear, or as I refer to it – faith in the wrong things, could that be bringing us into agreement with an evil covenant?

The Lord provided me with my own revelation on idolatry. I have, at times, turned to comfort food or a comical escape in entertainment to try and climb out of a black hole of depression. Sometimes the heaviness has been God's drawing me to prayer and intercession, especially if it is a heaviness that occurs out of the blue. God told me in one season that I was in idolatry because when I needed comfort during my empty nest syndrome, I turned to food and entertainment. Even in my sincere consistent relationship with God, I didn't even realize I was trying to fix myself. Addictions and sometimes indulgences can result in a form of idolatry. At the very heart of it, if the motive is turning to something else instead of Jesus to escape the pain, it is a replacement for God. This area has a fine line, and each person is different. It wasn't wrong for me to eat healthy desserts, etc.; it was how I used them. I repented and immediately started relying on God for my comfort instead, and my heavy darkness lifted. I have noticed that too much time spent on entertainment also causes a heaviness. He showed me how praise, worship, and thanksgiving would raise and strengthen me and increase my faith to cover me. Jesus created natural things to help us; Proverbs 17:22, "A merry heart doeth good *like* a medicine: ...." However, Jesus deserves the glory for it every time. Idolatry has become more common, whether joining in agreement with an actual false religious idol or things we are replacing God with – how we spend most of our leisure time.

As briefly mentioned before, times of sorrow, sadness, trauma, anger, pain, and any other negative emotion are target times for the enemy to attempt an entrance through our situation. If there are any legal rights to remain, he can then begin to set up a stronghold. Please, understand the intentions of this information. I aim to bring awareness and spark humility to reach for more freedom. I do not in any way want to create fear or rigid, legalistic obedience inspired by fear. I'm not saying one common sin will cause someone to be possessed or oppressed.

In Daniel 10, we see that Daniel had been fasting, and an angel appeared to give him the understanding of a vision. In Verse 8, Daniel states that his "...comeliness was turned in me into corruption...." It appears he felt unclean in the presence of the angel. The angel informs Daniel in Verse 12 that his words were heard the first day. In Verse 13, the angel had been withstood twenty-one days by the principality of Persia. Since Israel was in captivity, the proper procedure for atonement was probably not being made each year. Therefore, under the law of Moses in Leviticus 16:29, 30, Daniel was considered technically in sin. We see in Daniel 5:12;

6:10 that Daniel had an excellent spirit. However, the enemy will use whatever legal accusation works. Was the literal unatoned sin a legal element that delayed the answer in prayer?

Before I received the Holy Ghost, God answered many prayers. He hears us when we repent, so I know He is merciful and loves us even when we are in sin. We no longer depend on a fleshly priest to make atonement for our sins. However, I'm convinced that sin can still hinder certain prayers allowing the enemy to *delay* our blessings and answers.

Here are just a few scriptures concerning sin and its effects on prayer: Isaiah 59:1,2; Hebrews 11:6; 1 Peter 3:7, 12; James 1:6-8; 4:3-8; 5:16

Daniel was known for dissolving doubts in Daniel 5:16. The Hebrew translations of 08271 *shre'* [1] and 07001 *qtar* stand for *unraveling riddles* or *unraveling a knot*.[1] Suddenly, the Lord whispered to me, think of doubt like a knot tied in an electrical current or water hose. It hinders the flow and can even ruin that section over time. Doubt and unbelief can creep in like a brier during a trial without us even realizing it. Praise, the Word, prayer, and fasting will strengthen our faith and uproot doubt.

Isaiah 53:5 lets us know that Jesus paid the price for our sins, our healing, and our peace. Could the crown of thorns of Matthew 27:29 symbolize *peace* and victory over the battle in our minds? The enemy meant to mock Him from head to toe for being King, using a symbol of the original curse from Genesis 3:18. But the enemy was unaware this was giving Him authority in the spirit. Peace is ours in Jesus' Name!

CHAPTER 9
DELIVERANCE IN SCRIPTURE

Here is a quick reference for evil spirits mentioned during the time of Jesus.

Matthew	Mark	Luke	John	Acts
4:24	1:23-39	4:33-41	6:70	5:3, 16
7:22	3:11, 15, 22, 30	6:18	13:2, 27	8:7
8:16,17,23-34	5:2-18	7:21		10:38
9:32-34	6:7, 13	8:2, 27-39		13:8-12
10:1, 8	7:25-30	9:1, 38-50		16:16
12:22-45	9:17-29, 38, 39	10:17, 20		19:12-19
15:22, 28	16:9, 17	11:14-26		
16:23		13:16, 32		
17:14-21		22:3		

James 1:13-27 begins with a basic introduction of where spiritual warfare begins. In Chapter 2, he stresses the balance of faith and works. In Verse 17 of that chapter, he indicates that faith without works is dead (3498 <u>nekros</u> – *inactive.)*[1] In the following verses, it becomes even more apparent that there are supernatural undertones. James points out a wisdom he describes as earthly, sensual, and devilish:

<u>James 3:14-16</u> "But if ye have bitter envying and strife in your hearts, glory not, and lie not against the truth. This wisdom

descendeth not from above, but *is* earthly, sensual, devilish. For where envying and strife *is*, there *is* confusion and every evil work."

James 4:1 "From whence *come* wars {4171 *Polemos - warfare, battle, fight*}[1] and fightings among you? *come they* not hence, *even* of your lusts that war in your members?"

James 4:5-10 "Do ye think that the scripture saith in vain, The spirit that dwelleth in us lusteth to envy? But he giveth more grace. Wherefore he saith, God resisteth the proud, but giveth grace unto the humble. Submit yourselves therefore to God. Resist the devil, and he will flee from you. Draw nigh to God, and he will draw nigh to you. Cleanse *your* hands, *ye* sinners; and purify *your* hearts, *ye* double minded. Be afflicted, and mourn, and weep: let your laughter be turned to mourning, and *your* joy to heaviness. Humble yourselves in the sight of the Lord, and he shall lift you up."

Submit in the Greek – 5293 *hypotasso*,[1] from 5259 *hypo*,[1] and 5021 *tasso* meaning *to obey, be in subjection, cooperate – assuming responsibility*[1]

Resist in the Greek – 436 *anthistemi*[1] from
473 *anti*,[1] 2476 *histemi*,[1] 5087 *tithemi*,[1] and 2749 *keimai* - *to oppose, requital, covenant, weigh before judges, lay aside, put down, wear, or carry no longer, or breaking covenant with the devil* [1]

Afflicted in the Greek – 5003 *talaiporeo*[1] from 5007 *talanton*,[1] 5342 *phero*,[1] and 3984 *peira* – essentially defined – *to bring forward, carry, piercing through, and a trial or test* [1]

There are several instructions here: Submit to God, Resist the devil, draw nigh to God, cleanse your hands, purify your hearts, be afflicted, mourn, weep, etc. It is important also to note that the Greek word used for "doubleminded" is 1374 *dipsychos* – *two-spirited.*[1]

Then in the next chapter, James 5, the thought continues. Verse 15 mentions sickness and sins in the same verse:

<u>James 5:16</u> "Confess *your* faults one to another, and pray one for another, that ye may be healed. The effectual fervent prayer of a righteous man availeth much."

Confess – 1843 *exomologeo,*[1] 1537 *ek,*[1] 3670 *homologeo,*[1] 3056 *logos* – *to acknowledge, to profess that one will do something, to promise, out of, away from, covenant, concede, declare, case, suit at law*[1]

Faults – 3900 *paraptoma,*[1] 3895 *parapipto,*[1] 3844 *para,*[1] 4098 *pipto* – *a side slip, unintentional error, or transgression, offense, sin, trespass, wander, fall under judgment or condemnation, overcome by terror or grief, under the attack of an evil spirit, to lose authority*[1]

"*Healed* – 2390 *iaomai* – *to cure, heal, make whole, to free from errors and sins, to bring about salvation*"[1]

Admitting your sins, and praying one for another, that you may be free from sins sounds like spiritual deliverance to me. Could these scriptures have been more in reference to those who are sick spiritually, emotionally, and physically from a spiritual origin?

Physical healing was usually translated using the Greek word 2323 *therapeuo*[1] – the same word from which our English terms "therapeutic" and "therapy" are derived.

2390 *Iaomai*, meaning *healed*,[1] relates to freedom from sins, making it a perfect fit for James 5:16. The Bible occasionally references particular instances of sickness in connection with sin. (Matthew 9:2) However, that isn't always the case, as we saw in John 9:1-3, so we should never be quick to judge.

In 2 Corinthians 12:20 – 2 Corinthians 13:1-5, we see scripture indicating that certain members of the church at Corinth had some issues. Paul instructed them to examine and prove themselves in Verse 5. The Greek word "examine" is 3985 *peirazo*[1] from 3984 *peira*,[1] which is the root word we saw previously from the word "afflicted" in James 4:9.

Humbling and examining ourselves is scriptural. Believing that you cannot have an attachment after salvation is what I call the "once saved – always saved" version of Pentecost. This is not scriptural. We must not let tradition blind us from receiving more freedom. There are sincere believers struggling with thoughts and things that do not belong in them. There are those who once served God but, because of their silent struggles and not knowing they could receive more freedom, have fallen away. Freedom still awaits.

There are five verses about having an *evil spirit*, 20 verses relating to those who had *unclean spirits*, 24 concerning having a *devil*, and 37 that mention individuals having *devils*. If we just used the verses containing those four words alone, we have 86 verses about having an attachment! This stuff was a part of Jesus' daily ministry. (Isaiah 61:1; Luke 4:18-21)

According to the Old Testament, there was a connection to sin or the effects of sin and the third and fourth generations. But what if our ancestors continued the sins of their previous generations? There have been approximately 66ish generations since Jesus. With every generation, if continuing in sin from previous generations, the possibility of inheriting curses or attachments has increased. Could this be part of the reason sin has increased in the world? We, as humans, fail and are victims of failures, but Jesus' Name, Word, and Blood never fail.

CHAPTER 10
HEALING AND DELIVERANCE

Healing Versus Deliverance:

Years ago, five years into my new life as a Christian and before any other deliverance, I experienced a spirit of infirmity or sickness attacking my health. I felt strongly that the ailment was of a spiritual origin. At the same time, my pastor had seen a vision of a mass in my body. I had actual physical symptoms, and my immune system had taken a hit, but the red flag indicating that it was of a spiritual origin was the fear that came with it. It was not a typical concern or caution that naturally occurs with sickness, but instead an intense fear of being alone. As mentioned in my previous deliverance testimony, I have noticed that most evil attachments/ spirits do not travel alone. As that year progressed, I became increasingly discouraged because I believed I would be *healed*, only to leave the same way after each church service. It wasn't until right before my deliverance that the Lord revealed to me that an open window or legal right for this attachment was from thoughts that had been left unchecked. Once I understood this, I was then delivered from that spirit of infirmity. Healing began afterward. Had I known that I was harboring hidden sin and needed deliverance first, I could have been free from that troubling sickness much sooner. At that time, I didn't really understand the concept of what had happened. The deliverance wasn't frightening, but instead very freeing. Others even witnessed my countenance change as those attachments left. This revelation made me wonder how many people become discouraged while praying for healing when *repentance* and *deliverance* is the key.

As part of this concept was introduced in the last chapter, we will dive deeper. The following list of scriptures indicates that healing and deliverance were often mentioned together.

Matthew 4:24 "And his fame went throughout all Syria: and they brought unto him all sick people that were taken with divers diseases and torments, and those which were possessed with devils, and those which were lunatic, and those that had the palsy; and he healed them."

Matthew 9:32,33 mentions a deaf man possessed with a devil (This does NOT imply that all who are deaf have an evil spirit.)

Matthew 10:1, 8 Jesus gives the disciples power to cast out unclean spirits, heal every sickness and disease, raise the dead, etc.

Matthew 12:22 "Then was brought unto him one possessed with a devil, blind, and dumb: and he healed him, insomuch that the blind and dumb both spake and saw." (Verses 28, 29, 43-45 give further understanding about deliverance.)

Matthew 17:14-21; Mark 3:15; Mark 6:7; Mark 9:17-29

Mark 6:13 "And they cast out many devils, and anointed with oil many that were sick, and healed *them*."

Mark 16:15-18 The great commission

Luke 13:10-13,16 "And he was teaching in one of the synagogues on the sabbath. And, behold, there was a woman which had a spirit of infirmity eighteen years, and was bowed together, and could in no wise lift up *herself*. And when Jesus saw her, he called *her to him*, and said unto her, Woman, thou art loosed from thine infirmity. And he laid *his* hands on her: and immediately she was made straight, and glorified God." Verse 16 "And ought not this woman, being a daughter of Abraham, whom Satan hath bound, lo, these eighteen years, be loosed from this bond on the sabbath day?"

At that point, the Holy Ghost was not yet poured out, but to be considered "a daughter of Abraham," and the fact that they were in the synagogue points to a sincere worshipper. It wasn't the first instance of deliverance happening in a place of worship.

Luke 4:33-36, 39-41 (Note the interchangeable words used here for "unclean spirit" and "devil.") Jesus rebuked the fever in Simon's mother-in-law in Verse 39, much like rebuking the devil.

Luke 6:18 "And they that were vexed with unclean spirits: and they were healed."

Luke 8:2 "And certain women, which had been healed of evil spirits and infirmities, Mary called Magdalene, out of {575 apo – *separation, departing, destroyed union or fellowship, off, away, cessation, reversal* [Note: the prefix to many other Greek words mentioned previously]}[1] whom went seven devils,"

(Two more women were mentioned by name, Joanna, and Susanna, in Verse 3) Later in this same chapter, Luke 8:27-39 tells the story of Legion. He is also mentioned in Mark 5. Considering and comparing these descriptions, we might notice a storm preceding this situation. Those spirits preferred to remain in the past or where dead things were. Maybe this man had family that was among those buried in that place. He was indecently exposed, had unusual strength, cried, and cut himself (melancholy and suicidal.) It is heartbreaking to imagine, but those details are common even today. The devils asked that Jesus would not command them to go out into the deep (Greek 12 *abyssos* – meaning *bottomless, pit, the abyss*.)[1] After the devils went from the man to the herd of swine, the pigs ran violently down a steep place into the lake and were choked. Pigs can swim. I'm convinced that those spirits wanted to remain in that territory.

It is crucial to think of those delivered with compassion, not judgment or fear. Most likely, the man known for Legion had his own name. Think of the power of Jesus in that man's desperation! He could still overcome thousands of devils and run to Jesus in his miserable state! Matthew 8:23-34 has a similar account.

Philip went to Samaria and preached Christ in Acts 8:5-24. The people received what he said and saw the miracles that were accomplished. Unclean spirits left many; palsies and lame were healed, there was great joy, and they were baptized but had not received the Holy Ghost yet, according to Verses 15-17. If evil spirits automatically leave when you receive the Holy Spirit, would the deliverance ministered by Philip in Verse 7 have been necessary? Also, it seems Simon the sorcerer wasn't automatically delivered when he believed and was baptized in Verse 13. In Verses 21-24, his bondage still seems apparent. This proves that *just* believing and baptism isn't an automatic ticket into heaven. Believing and baptism are significant first steps, however. (Acts 19:1-6)

Have you ever sinned since receiving God's Spirit? The answer is most likely *yes* because flesh tends to make mistakes. Being tempted isn't a sin, but giving into temptation is. The power of God is strong enough to make us perfect in Him.

If everyone isn't completely healed from every physical and emotional ailment immediately upon salvation, then isn't it possible not to be delivered entirely as well? Jesus destroyed the curse of sin for us, but we still live in our bodies made of flesh and blood in this world full of sin. The Holy Spirit does not make us immune to sin, and thankfully, His Spirit doesn't leave us every time we sin or have a bad attitude!

Once again, not every situation or sickness results from an evil spirit or attachment. The Lord has revealed to me in prayer during certain situations natural remedies to use for an ailment, and to my knowledge, the condition wasn't evil spirit induced. He even created plants and trees with healing properties. We are human, and sometimes we catch viruses. Sometimes our bodies need detoxing, or maybe we are just reaping the unhealthy meals or unhealthy lifestyles we have sown. Be prayerful and discerning, asking God for wisdom. Common sense says that our bodies will break down naturally as we age. These things are not spiritual but natural and a part of life.

CHAPTER 11
THE WHERE

Where exactly does deliverance take place? My intentions are not to spark debates concerning exactly where evil attachments reside. Although after asking the Lord in prayer where most unclean spirits are attached, I felt very strongly that the Lord told me *our flesh*. I'm convinced this includes the mind and emotions. Immediately, I was then reminded of some scriptures which support this idea. (Romans 7:5-23; 8:1-13; 13:12-14; 1 Corinthians 6:16, 17; 2 Corinthians 7:1; 12:7; Galatians 5:16-26; Galatians 6:8; Ephesians 2:2,3; Colossians 2:11-18; 2 Peter 2:10; 1 John 2:16; Jude 1:7, 8, 23) (2 Corinthians 10:3; and Ephesians 6:12 are worded differently but not contradicting in that the spiritual battle is not fought in the flesh, as in a human being against a human being. And it cannot be won by the flesh because we are powerless without Jesus against the spirit world.)

As I mentioned briefly before, "flesh," "body," "soul," and "spirit" could be interchanged many times in scripture. The metaphorical "heart" and "mind" indicate our feelings, intentions, thoughts, and emotions. Determining the fine line between the flesh /carnality, soul, and what is spirit can be challenging. Hebrews 4:12 lets us know there is a difference between "soul" and "spirit." Galatians 4:6 mentions that the Holy Spirit is sent forth into our hearts. The Greek word for "heart" is also used in conjunction with the "soul." Our "mind" is also connected with the "soul" in Greek and Hebrew translation definitions.

Interestingly, my daughter pointed out one day that evil spirits entered pigs, mentioned previously in Matthew 8:31, 32, Mark 5:12-13, and Luke 8:30-33. Did they attach to the pigs' flesh or spirit? Does it matter? How does an evil spirit remain on cursed items and occult items? I honestly don't think evil spirits care where they dwell as long as there is access to a human being. The Holy Spirit lives inside us spiritually, preventing demonic access to wherever He reigns. If a part of our flesh, mind, soul, or emotions is not surrendered to the Holy Spirit, that could be open territory. Romans 7:20 ends the verse with this phrase that indicates that sin dwells inside of us, "....but sin that dwelleth in me." If sin is the doorway to an evil spirit, then it seems most likely that the evil spirit dwells wherever the sin is.

Sin, the gateway for unclean attachments, looks at wounds as opportunities, whether they are physical, emotional, or spiritual. Proverbs 18:14 mentions a wounded spirit. Psalms 109:22 mentions a wounded heart.

Because this spiritual battle is often mirrored in our natural realm, we must remember that we are not fighting people. Evil spirits are very deceptive; if they can distract us, causing us to fight each other, they win. It is also essential to be kind and compassionate when publicly challenged with morals as we stand our ground. A debate, argument, or critical judgment is not a wise outreach or deliverance method. We battle hate with love. If our methods are judgment and fear, then the results will be judgmental individuals motivated to serve God entirely out of fear. Let's use wisdom in deliverance and not judgment.

Arguments over where, how, and why aren't necessary; *freedom* should be the targeted result. My goal here is not to decide if an attachment is a form of oppression, demonization, a curse, or a stronghold; however, I will provide definitions for comparisons.

A <u>stronghold</u> is often described as a fortress or a place of defense connected directly to your mind and thoughts. It implies a spiritual structure of power built over time due to thoughts and possibly reinforced by an unclean spirit. Strongholds must be broken down.

<u>2 Corinthians 10:3-5</u> "For though we walk in the flesh, we do not war after the flesh: (For the weapons of our warfare *are* not carnal, but mighty through God to the pulling down {2506 *kathairesis n. – destruction*}[1] of strong holds;) {3794 *ochyroma – castle, fortress*}[1] Casting down {2507 *kathaireo v.– demolish*}[1] imaginations, and every high thing {5313 *hypsoma – elevated barrier, wall of defense*}[1] that exalteth itself against the knowledge of God, and bringing into captivity every thought to the obedience of Christ;"

If a stronghold is a mindset that has been reinforced and built over time, it might take time to demolish it, but on the flip side, couldn't we strengthen our minds with scripture?

A <u>curse</u> is evil spoken over someone and activated due to sin. (Deuteronomy 11:26-28; 28:15-68) Many generational curses come from the sins of ancestors through our bloodline. These result from sin/ disobedience that has not been repented of or broken. (Genesis 3:14-19; 8:20-22; 9:22-25; 12:3; Exodus 20:5, 6; 34:7; Leviticus 26:40-42; Nehemiah 1:4-9; 9:1-3; Proverbs 26:2; 28:27; Lamentations 5:7)

Curses can be broken and removed, resulting in manifestations, sometimes similar to evil spirits that leave our bodies. This could be from the evil spirits that are assigned to make those curses effective. Sometimes an evil attachment will not depart until a generational curse is broken.

Acts 10:38 is the only KJV example of the use of "<u>oppressed</u>" in terms of being oppressed by the devil. Greek translation – "2616 <u>katadynasteuo</u> v. *To exercise harsh control over one, to use one's power against one*"[1] from 1413 <u>dynastes</u> – *prince, great authority* [1]

Greek for "<u>possessed</u>" in the KJV, "1139 <u>Daimonizomai</u> meaning *to be under the power of a demon.*"[1] from "1142 <u>Daimon</u>- *a demon, a god, a goddess, an inferior deity, an evil spirit.*"[1] Notice the words "*god*" and "*goddess*" used in this definition; as I briefly mentioned before, this definition gives us a perspective on the connection between gods/goddesses/idols/ demons/fallen angels.

1139 Daimonizomai[1] was the Greek blanket term used for someone dealing with an evil attachment, whether considered oppression or possession.

Maybe you have heard the expression "soul ties," which implies souls joined together. It isn't a biblical term but a concept that probably stemmed from 1 Samuel 18:1 in the story of Jonathan and David, who were very close. The word "knit" in this verse comes from the Hebrew word 07194 *qashar* – *tie, bind*.[1] This type of unity can be God-ordained and a tremendous blessing; however, this can also take place with toxic relationships.

In the New Testament, Corinth was a city historically known for its idolatry and specific sins connected with this practice, such as fornication. These sins were mentioned in letters to the church. Not only is fornication and sexual immorality a sin, but according to 1 Corinthians 6:15-20, it is a sin *against* the body. When two are joined, they become one. (Genesis 2:24) If you have joined yourself with another physically, outside of marriage, not only is that sin, but you are also opening yourself to their attachments and possibly soul ties.

1 Corinthians 6:18 "Flee fornication. Every sin that a man doeth is without {1622 *ektos* – *exterior, outside*}[1] the body; but he that committeth fornication sinneth against {"1519 *eis* – *into, unto, to, towards"*}[1] his own body."

1 Peter 2:11 "Dearly beloved, I beseech *you* as strangers and pilgrims, abstain from fleshly lusts, which war against the soul;"

In exploring the idea of where attachments can be, I found an interesting article posted in *Scientific American* about our gut's "second brain." Also known as the enteric nervous system, it is made up of intricate and complicated neurons that control gut behavior independently of the brain. Scientists were amazed to discover around 90 percent of the fibers of the vagus nerve send information *from* our gut brain *to* the brain in our head. They believe our emotions are greatly affected by our second brain. This explains why our stomachs can feel knotted during stress or the common "butterflies" feeling during excitement.[6] It is likely this was known in Biblical times from the use of a term found in various scriptures. The term "bowels" was often described as the seat of emotions or deeper feelings. Could this be why many attachments seem to feel as if they are leaving our stomach area? Maybe they are attached to our emotions or "second brain." (Genesis 43:30; Lamentations 1:20; Philemon 1:7, 20; 1 John 3:17) Romans 8:7 has an interesting definition for the Greek term for "mind" in the phrase "carnal mind" – 5427 *phronema*[1] with the root 5424 *phren* meaning the *midriff, diaphragm,* heart, mind, and *feelings.*[1] Also, I find it interesting in Numbers 33:55 that the dwellers in

---

[6] *Think Twice: How the Gut's "Second Brain" Influences Mood and Well-Being.* Adam Hadhazy (02/12/2010)
https://www.scientificamerican.com/article/gut-second-brain/

which Israel didn't drive out became "pricks" and "thorns" in their *eyes* and *sides*, vexing (binding) them. I find the word choice, "pricked," used in both Psalms 73:21 and Acts 2:37 also interesting. We can either be pricked by a sword (God's Word) or by a thorn (the enemy's word.) The Word cleanses by piercing us to remove the bad. It can provide nourishment, bringing light and life. The thorn entangles us and wounds us with a poison bringing darkness and death.

My theory for most sins that were considered an *abomination* in the Old Testament is that those sins were automatic openings for demonic attachments. This happened because those sins united the person through the contract of sin with a demon, whether as a curse or a spiritual attachment. There is also an indication of this concept in Leviticus 18:29. There is one scripture reference for individual deliverance in the Old Testament, in the instance where David played for Saul to ease his affliction from a spirit (1 Samuel 16:14-16, 23.) Here are a few more instances where *spirits* are mentioned in the Old Testament: 1 Samuel 28:12, 13; 1 Kings 22:19-23; Isaiah 11:2; 61:3; Hosea 4:12

In the New Testament, Evil spirits are cast out in Jesus' Name, and this was also a sign of the Messiah. (Isaiah 61:1, 2 - Luke 4:18-21; Matthew 12:28) Jesus weakened the principalities over certain areas by removing many evil spirits.

So, to answer the question, *Where* does deliverance take place? The answer depends on where the spiritual attachment is. It is often attached to our flesh or bloodline, so manifestations might occur as it leaves, which I previously addressed. I don't think we should be concerned about *where*. Many spiritual things are a mystery. The Holy Ghost can be wherever it chooses and is not at all threatened or limited by an unclean attachment.

Another side to the question is: where the actual deliverance session should occur. The primary focus in each situation is freedom. No one should ever feel judged, embarrassed, pressured, exploited, or afraid. I understand that opportunities can be spontaneous for deliverance. Public deliverance is humbling, powerful, and can cause others to manifest. Depending on the season of the assembly, sometimes the wisest location for complete and thorough deliverance can be scheduled in a more private and controlled setting. This is ideal with an experienced team and poses fewer distractions for everyone. If the person needing deliverance becomes sick or violent, this can be very distracting, especially for first-time visitors in the congregation. However, it should not be pushed into the back room because it is embarrassing. Every church's culture is different. One deliverance could trigger more deliverances and then spark a revival. Jesus didn't always do deliverance in private.

As in any altar situation, *one voice* is better than several when ministering to that person. If one person is ministering to the seeker in words, such as leading them in prayer, if I feel something, I prefer to tell the one ministering rather than confuse the seeker with several voices. It can be frustrating and almost comical when several sincere altar workers pray with one individual in contradiction. One might tell them to "let go," while another tells that person to "hold on."

Once, I was a spectator in a discouraging deliverance session with someone I did not feel was manifesting sickness because of a demon. Afterward, in prayer, the Lord told me that if I questioned whether it was an actual sickness, I should try binding the spirit causing illness. Manifestation should not be allowed the power to hinder or distract from the deliverance process. Freedom is the goal. The enemy will always try to restrict that, if possible. Sometimes what appears to be a manifestation is really just a physical condition, or the person could be in an altered state from substance abuse. The more informed, sensitive, and discerning we become, the better. I am not implying that you should *attempt* to bind every manifestation. It is important to let God lead you.

Deliverance is rarely like Hollywood scary movies. Complete deliverance doesn't have to be done in one day. If there are multiple attachments, it is okay to space out deliverance as you feel ready. You may only discover another spirit after one is removed. I do believe discernment is important in this ministry because all spirits do not manifest or leave in the same manner. Because circumstances and individuals are different, it is necessary to be sensitive to discern if the spirit has truly gone.

Matthew 11:2-5 mentions John the Baptist's last question about the Messiah. One day, while reading Isaiah, I noticed that Jesus' answer to John was similar to the scriptures I read in Isaiah 42, especially Verses 16-21 that foretold the Messiah. I can see how the miraculous healing of the blind and deaf was literal and figurative. With the growing popularity of deliverance, healings will become more frequent in the last days, much like during Jesus' ministry.

Demons are no doubt aware of various cultures. If someone from the U.S.A. visited another country, they could more easily discern a manifestation of an attachment there. Whereas in their own country, the spirits have learned how to blend subtly. Camouflage now appears under the guise of a "lighter" shade of darkness. We know that Jesus is the true Light, John 8:12. Darkness is often "rebranded" today as light. Notice in that same chapter how Jesus was teaching in the temple, and in John 8:32, He told "Abraham's seed" that the truth would make them free. In Verse 33, they replied that they were never in bondage to any man. Jesus was trying to let them know that they were *spiritually* in bondage. They didn't get it, so He told them plainly in Verse 44 that their father was the devil. Their response in Verse 52 was to accuse Jesus of "having" a devil. The Greek word 2192 <u>echo</u> means *to be joined, to have, or own.*[1] Instead of humbly examining themselves, that group refused to let go of their imperfect religious theology and attack the Deliverer.

The enemy's agenda has not changed. There are new scenarios and methods, but the basics follow the same patterns.

The word "supernatural" can represent a variety of things now. However, I am convinced that the Lord has placed a natural attraction for the supernatural inside of every human being, however minuscule or misplaced it may be at times. If you are unconvinced, check out the various articles mentioned in the article *Occulture Trend Report: Selling the Mystical to a Millennial Market*. This *Shutterstock* report was based on searches suggesting a growing interest in alt-faiths, the occult, and astrology. The data indicated a +525% rise in searches for "magic" while also seeing an increase of +289% in searches for "spiritual." With popular entertainment targeting these generations, trendy occult images of "magic" and "spiritual" have increased their appeal to the "woke" Millennials and Gen Z consumers.[7]

The number of Americans who claimed to be witches and/or practicing Wicca religious rituals increased from 8,000 in 1990 to 1.5 million in 2018, in a study conducted by Trinity College. The data also provided information that there were 340,000 Pagans in the U.S. in 2008. Author Julie Roys emailed comments to The Christian Post in October 2018, saying, "The rejection of Christianity has left a void that people, as inherently spiritual beings, will seek to fill. Plus, Wicca has effectively repackaged witchcraft for

---

[7] *Occulture Trend Report: Selling the Mystical to a Millennial Market.* Grace Fussell (01/29/20)
https://www.shutterstock.com/blog/occulture-mystical-design-trend

millennial consumption. No longer is witchcraft and paganism satanic and demonic; it's a 'pre-Christian tradition' that promotes 'free thought' and 'understanding' of earth and nature." The article in a 2018 issue of *Newsweek* also stated that despite previous findings, Christianity still dominates 70% of the country's religious population - taken from the Pew Research Center in 2018.[8] In reading the comments below this article, I noticed several disgruntled readers who found it offensive for those who practice paganism and Wicca to be placed in the same category as satanic and demonic. I think it is wise to research traditions and practices before engaging in or continuing with them. Wicca and paganism historically can trace their roots to the same gods and goddesses or fallen angels from which Satanism also originated.

Over the years, Hollywood and media have made merchandise of the demonic, either by capitalizing on the belief that evil spirits are terrifying or by creating an alluring and glamorous view of a dark fantasy world. It has also become popular to investigate the hidden story behind "villains." While it brings insight into understanding someone's hidden trauma, we should make sure this mindset doesn't lead to normalizing and validating wrong behavior.

---

[8] *Number of Witches Rises Dramatically Across U.S. As Millennials Reject Christianity.* Benjamin Fearnow (11/18/18 at 10:17 am Est.) Culture Source Information:
 https://www.newsweek.com/witchcraft-wiccans-mysticism-astrology-witches-millenials-pagans-religion-1221019

On the other spectrum, much of the religious world does not discuss the supernatural. The stigma created by superstition and/or misrepresentation isn't a great outreach tool. Much of society has been exposed to the dramatized version of the dark side, but little is spoken from those who actually oppose this dark side. Let's face it; the enemy has spent years through history studying us to make sure we are entirely deceived. If our adversary can keep us frightened and superstitious from lack of knowledge, we become powerless in the arena of spiritual warfare and deliverance.

The dark agenda of deception is often aimed at those affected emotionally by trauma, such as loss. Avenues like hypnosis, psychics, energy healing, and meditation have become therapy alternatives. Do not be deceived by these tricks of the enemy. Any form of altering the mind or interacting in the spirit realm that God has not initiated is dangerous. The popular term "energy" has become a preferred way to describe things we can't see but can feel. The only "energy" we should interact with is the power of Jesus. Jesus and His Word are the only things we are to meditate on and consult. (Deuteronomy 6:6-9; 18: 10-12; Joshua 1:8; Psalms 1:2; 119:15, 24, 48; Philippians 4:8) God, as Creator of the universe, is the Source of all power and, therefore, has all authority over every spirit and principality. I'm thankful He provides us with angelic assistance and His manifest presence faithfully to combat every enemy assignment.

Notice in Acts 19 what transpired after the seven sons of Sceva tried to cast out an evil spirit and were attacked in Verses 13-16. That circumstance caused many to be stirred about the name of Jesus:

Acts 19:18,19 "And many that believed came, and confessed, and shewed their deeds. Many of them also which used curious arts brought their books together, and burned them before all *men*: and they counted the price of them, and found *it* fifty thousand *pieces* of silver."

Interesting points in these two verses are the meanings of those words that were used for what the people did in response to discovering the power of Jesus' Name.

Confessed:1843 *exomologeo*[1] – *acknowledge, declare, profess.*[1]
Shewed: 312 *anangello* – *announce, report, declare, speak;*[1] from the basis of 303 *ana* – *reversal, amidst;*[1] and 32 *angelos* – *a messenger, an angel, bring tidings.*[1]
Deeds: 4234 *praxis* – *transaction, deal.*[1]

The Bible does not say that all unclean/evil spirits must be terrifying or extremely harmful. As we have seen before, they can be as unassuming as a common negative "personality" trait.

Personality tests are a constant trend in helping us navigate each other and ourselves. Still, we should avoid getting caught up in classifying what or who we are. We should be ever-growing and improving as the Lord purifies and refines us for His benefit.

How do we truly know if we are exhibiting a negative natural, learned behavior or if it is a spiritual manifestation? This was briefly touched on before, but I'm providing a few more red flags to help you identify some common symptoms of spiritual attachments. You do not have to exhibit all of these symptoms to have an attachment. My disclaimer is that some of these symptoms can result from actual medical conditions, as well, that should be treated by a trusted medical professional. Because a spirit can cause physical symptoms, it can be hard to detect it as a spiritual issue unless there are other indications. Also, if you currently receive medication or medical treatment for anything, including PTSD, please do NOT discontinue anything unless you first consult your physician. Immediately discontinuing medication can result in serious side effects or harm to yourself and others.

Symptoms of demonic attachments include but are not limited to: an extended continuation of negative emotions, fantasizing or extended daydreaming, experiencing paranormal activity, evil or invasive thoughts, voices - whether audible or reoccurring as unwanted thoughts, a desire to cause harm to yourself or others, involuntary cursing especially during church services, knowing things before they happen without/before being a Holy Spirit filled believer, frequent nightmares, sleep paralysis, anger issues, addictions, a high level of fear, memory loss or unaccounted time, uncontrollable negative "personality" traits or disorders, eating disorders or obsessive tendencies, unexplained seizures or convulsions, lack of control, promiscuity, perversion, alternative lifestyles, feeling drawn to dark entertainment, shame, avoiding eye contact, intense envy and jealousy, tendencies toward drama, and/or gossip, unexplained illnesses, confusion, self-sabotage, an unexplained feeling of opposition to certain types of people, racism, prejudice, suspicion, paranoia, dominance, manipulation, opposition to the idea of deliverance, and finally a dislike of scripture, preaching, prayer, or Christian music in general.

This list of the most common symptoms is not complete. If you have ever experienced any of these, it will not hurt to repent and verbally renounce these symptoms or any sins associated with these if you haven't already. If words were involved in the sin, retract your sinful words. I have also felt at times to ask God to remove the sins from my record. The following scripture speaks of "conversation," but its Greek word refers to "conduct."

Ephesians 4:22, 23 "That ye put off concerning the former conversation the old man, which is corrupt according to the deceitful lusts; And be renewed in the spirit of your mind;" (underlined emphasis, mine)

This is a great example where the Greek word 659 *apotithemi – cast off, lay aside, or down*[1] is used in the form of *put off* and later in Verse 25 in the form of *putting away*. Paul was speaking to the Ephesian *church*. In Verse 27, "Neither give place to the devil." is stated in the middle of Paul advising the church on morals.

Give – 1325 *didomi – grant or permit*[1]
Place – 5117 *topos – home, portion, and power*[1]

We must not grant permission for legal occupancy or authority to the devil. Chapter 6 of Ephesians mentions the whole armor of God. Verse 12:

"For we wrestle not against flesh and blood, but against principalities, {746 *arche* – *chief, ruler* – *angels and demons,*}[1] against powers, against the rulers of the darkness of this world, against spiritual wickedness in high *places.*"

The word for "wrestle" in the previous verse is the Greek word 3823 *pale*[1] – which references another form of the word 906 *ballo*, meaning *to throw or cast out.*[1] – the root of the familiar 1544 *ekballo,*[1] the Greek word commonly used in the gospels for "casting out evil spirits."

The "whole armor of God" is essential to God's covering and protection. It is mentioned in Ephesians 6:14-17 and has several elements. The angle I'm considering here is openings for the enemy since a battle with the enemy is the focus of that letter to the Ephesian church.

The pieces of spiritual armor protect our most vulnerable areas. The <u>shield of faith</u> is significant because it can protect any area from attack by covering it with faith and prayer. The <u>sword</u> is valuable because each time you use the Word of God, you use the voice of Jesus' blood. This powerful fact defeats the enemy – <u>Our loins</u> – spiritual reproduction, identity, and strength – are affected if truth is attacked. If the <u>helmet of salvation</u> is attacked, our mind

– thoughts, and spiritual senses, such as vision, hearing, and speech, will suffer. If the attack is against the <u>breastplate of righteousness</u> – our heart and other vital organs are at risk. And finally, if the <u>preparation of the gospel of peace</u> – our walk, *balance*, destination, purpose, and mobility are under attack.

A special note about our feet being shod with the preparation of the gospel (tidings or good news) of peace (a covenant of safety and well-being.) Feet in the Old Testament relate to promises, ownership, victory, stumbling, and curses. True peace is something the enemy cannot duplicate. The Hebrew word for "peace" is 07965 *shalom*,[1] derived from 07999 *shalam*, meaning *to be safe or in* a *covenant of peace*.[1] True peace is an alliance or covenant with the Creator. We, as soldiers, are to be ready also to be messengers broadcasting the covenant of peace and salvation.

2 Timothy 2:3-5 were important instructions for Timothy as a soldier for Jesus. Note the word choice to "strive lawfully," used in Verse 5.

Another important note: To remove the armor, you must first lay down the sword and shield. We must daily keep the Word of God and faith close.

With this concept in mind, the Watch and Pray commands are more understandable. If the idea behind this is protection against the enemy, then the mindset that we are all automatically protected is wrong. God's Spirit is all-powerful, but if nothing can ever overcome us (living in the flesh) in an attack, for what are we watching? Why are we instructed to put on the whole armor? Romans, through Revelations, are written to churches and believers. How often do we see instructions and corrections in those letters? We cannot ever work our way into Heaven. However, prayer, good works, faith, and being watchful are all part of cultivating a relationship with God, who wants to have a relationship with us.

Matthew 24:42 "Watch therefore: for ye know not what hour your Lord doth come."

1 Thessalonians 5:6 "Therefore let us not sleep, as *do* others; but let us watch and be sober."

Hebrews 13:17 "…for they watch for your souls…."

1 Peter 5:8 "Be sober, be vigilant…."

More references: Matthew 24:43; 25:13; Mark 13:33-37; Luke 12:37-39; 21:36; 1 Corinthians 16:13; Ephesians 6:18; Colossians 4:2; 2 Timothy 4:5; 1 Peter 4:7; Jude 1:21; Revelation 3:2

Without His Spirit and Word, we are unarmed. Do not be discouraged when you stumble in the flesh. If you have His Spirit, you have the promise of 1 John 4:4. (Micah 7:8)

CHAPTER 12
FIRSTHAND DELIVERANCE

I mentioned in Chapter 1 that during my deliverance from selfishness and timidity, I experienced a vision or flashback. It revealed to me the open door where selfishness, timidity, and other spirits first became attached.

When I was very young, I received instruction one evening from a television show, during a children's program timeslot, on how to attempt psychokinesis or telekinesis – the ability to move objects with one's mind. I was not raised to attend church, but even if I had, I doubt I would have known at that age that the action was wrong. Enticed with curiosity, I felt challenged to move an item by following the instructions and was so amazed that it worked! I told my mother, who was busy cooking nearby, but her lack of positive reinforcement left me discouraged. I knew she was busy but probably also didn't believe me. After trying it a few more times, I stopped.

This scene from my childhood was the flashback I had experienced during my deliverance. I remember having vivid nightmares around that same time in my childhood, and I suddenly became terrified of sleeping alone. Interestingly, during this time, my best friend at school invited me to my first church service. Could the enemy have been trying to prevent me from experiencing God at a young age?

As I grew older, it isn't surprising that I became curious about the supernatural unknown and began immersing myself in ghost stories and mythology. In the 1980s, the paranormal had grown in popularity with various movies and books. I studied and read every book I could find on the subject, but since the internet was not yet available, my resources were limited. I recall reading a book referencing the complexities of time and the paranormal. While reading that book, I became very sick. I didn't see the connection at first but noticed oddly that I would improve when I stopped reading it. At first, I thought it was a coincidence, so I attempted to continue reading it a few more times, only to get sick each time. Frustrated, I finally decided not to finish the book and *instantly* recovered.

I had friends who were also curious about the supernatural. The challenges and adrenaline from the fear were appealing. We tried various forms of divination, attempted automatic writing, and decided to hold a séance on my 13th birthday. I remember being disappointed that no one witnessed anything during the séance. It wasn't until a few weeks later that I began to witness unexplained occurrences and apparitions. It became terrifying. I hadn't realized that my participation and interest in the paranormal was not only a sin but had now opened a serious spiritual door with legal grounds of attack from those spirits with which I had become so curious. The activity was not from actual ghosts of people; they were demons/evil spirits disguising themselves. It was no longer a fun and exciting curiosity, and I eventually removed all items and books associated with the paranormal. (Acts 19:19) My friends also seemed unaware that the Bible opposed this behavior. Even though they had all been sincere denominal churchgoers, I don't think those topics were ever discussed at their churches. Until my mid-teens, what little I had known about Jesus or the Bible, I had mostly read in a Bible storybook and was unaware that my actions were not pleasing to God. (Galatians 5:19-21; Leviticus 19:31; Leviticus 20:6)

The attachment of witchcraft I had joined myself with while partaking in those activities had never been addressed, and told to leave. God is not a respecter of persons, and even though I had been ignorant of the sins I had committed at the time and stopped those actions, it did not prevent me from remaining bound. I received the Holy Ghost about five years later. Looking back, I could see how if I had experienced deliverance from demonic attachments during the night of my conversion, I might have been too confused or embarrassed to return to church. At that time, there was a stigma surrounding that, and the deliverance ministry was not necessarily understood or popular in my location. This is one reason why I do not believe every attachment automatically leaves. New converts who know nothing, except the world's view of supernatural, might be too freaked out to continue after one deliverance.

God knew I was desperate to receive His Spirit. To the best of my knowledge, I had repented silently in my head, and then as Romans 8:38, 39 states, nothing separated me from His love, not even *principalities* or *powers*. It was as if the Lord embraced me despite all of the ugly. I received the Holy Ghost with the evidence of speaking in other tongues and then, twelve days later, was baptized in Jesus' Name. I didn't continue experimenting with the dark side of the unknown after Jesus found me, not because I wasn't drawn to it but because the Lord revealed it was wrong. So, the spirit/spirits were neglected, starved, no longer entertained, and weakened. It was *years* after my conversion before I was delivered from the spirit of witchcraft and a familiar spirit.

Before those spirits left me, certain manifestations happened. Witchcraft and the familiar spirit were attached to my mind/flesh, affecting my mind and flesh when leaving. Sudden feelings and thoughts of hopelessness, confusion, thoughts of suicide, and darkness attacked my mind all at once during that deliverance. Those were thoughts and feelings I rarely experienced and only when I was at my weakest. I had to bind the confusion and hopelessness to continue the deliverance.

Occasional paranormal activity is another symptom of having those attachments. If you experience any of the symptoms I have mentioned, consider the possibility that witchcraft might be the culprit. Do NOT dabble with darkness! If you have and have not experienced deliverance, repented, and/or renounced it, it is likely still there. Even if you don't feel it could still be attached, there is no harm in repenting and renouncing things like that from your past. If you have not been associated with witchcraft but have symptoms of it in your life, it could stem from an outside source of an attack or a generational curse. Unfortunately, I have seen this happen to fellow believers due to another praying and speaking against them.

Many of the spirits that I was first delivered from stemmed from that open door of witchcraft, and interestingly they seemed to depart in two's, which then exposed and revealed the next two as if they had accumulated in layers. There were several more attachments that were exposed. Some were generational curses. I believe God allowed this process to give me more understanding and insight.

During my repentance time in prayer, I began asking God to reveal any unclean spirits that lingered. I asked Him to show me what to repent of to remove any legal rights. Sometimes a proper descriptive name would come to my mind, and if I wasn't sure of its definition, I would look it up in the dictionary. I would then repent for whatever brought it into my life and command it to leave. I took note of the various manifestations and used the knowledge to recognize those spirits when helping others through deliverance.

One generational curse prevented me from opening my mouth as soon as I addressed it. I had to stop, regroup, take authority over, and bind it from restricting my mouth. That is why it is easier to have another help you in deliverance. None of those instances were scary, just humbling. My lack of knowledge at the time was frustrating, but the Holy Spirit led me every step of the way. I have felt to break several generational curses that would come to mind during prayer. Once I felt strongly to tell a spirit connected with a generational curse to restore what it had stolen from our family.

Deliverance can even be done over the phone. I wouldn't recommend it as an ideal way, though God has allowed me to do this. However, it is easier to accomplish this on a face-to-face call so that you can see what is happening.

It all may sound very unconventional if you are unfamiliar with this ministry, but it is real. Deliverance is a very humbling experience and something that no one wants to imagine themselves to need, but if you are feeling yourself in any way opposed to this subject, ask yourself: Why would God be opposed to thorough, sincere repentance and searching ourselves to draw closer to Him?

God is not opposed to delivering us from evil. That request is seen in the Lord's Prayer. What would be the purpose of the enemy wanting to trick us into believing a Christian could be bound? I could see, however, where the enemy would love to *blind* us to the truth that everyone is subject to the possibility of needing deliverance – saved or unsaved. To clarify once again, just because someone has a demon, that does not mean they are unsaved or are "possessed" or owned by demons. Christians might be bound or occupied but not owned. Understanding that Jesus' blood has all power, we can overcome fear and misconceptions of this subject.

<u>Luke 24:47</u> "And that repentance and remission {"859 *aphesis – freedom, pardon, deliverance, forgiveness, liberty, release from bondage or imprisonment, remission of the penalty,*"[1] from 863 *aphiemi - to send away, bid depart, expire, disregard, omit*}[1] of sins should be preached in his name among all nations, beginning at Jerusalem."

The blood of Jesus is what gives us remission of sins. (Matthew 26:28; Hebrews 9:22; 10:14-18) We apply His blood through repentance, baptism (Mark 1:4; Luke 3:3; Acts 2:38), and through faith (Acts 10:43; Romans 3:25), but if we disregard it, we aren't letting it cover our sins. It is similar to having a wound and knowing about medication for that wound but not receiving or applying it. Just because we have a prescription for healing salve doesn't mean the written prescription will help our wound. The salve must be received and applied.

Blood has a Voice:

In Matthew 6:13 and Luke 11:4 of the Lord's prayer, the same word for "deliver" is used both times in the prayer phrase, "deliver us from evil." It is not the most common Greek word used for this concept.

(4506 *rhyomai – from the idea of a current, to rush or draw, rescue – deliver or deliverer.*[1] Its associated roots in the Greek: "4482 *rheo – to flow*,"[1] and 4511 *rhysis – a flow of blood.*)[1]

If blood has a voice, as in Genesis 4:10, then when deliverance is happening, the blood of Jesus is speaking over that situation. His blood has THE voice, the voice of authority, the final voice. His blood is flowing to deliver, and that concept triggered the thought of the scripture that speaks of another voice that can rejoice and speak on our behalf:

James 2:13 "For he shall have judgment without mercy, that hath shewed no mercy; and mercy rejoiceth against judgment."

Mercy has a *voice*. Mercy and forgiveness cannot be separated. I do not think it is a coincidence that the verse just above the delivering part of the Lord's prayer is about forgiveness. If you find yourself stuck in a trial or hitting a wall in prayer, maybe unforgiveness is holding up progress. Unforgiveness can sneak in and lodge undetected, like a forgotten thorn under the skin. There may be discomfort initially, but you may get used to it. You may even become numb and convince yourself you are justified for feeling that way, but unforgiveness is a sin. It will cause a break in the hedge while preventing deliverance, healing, and salvation from happening if it remains.

Matthew 6:12 "And forgive {863 *aphiemi – send away, depart, divorce, expire, remit, omit*}[1] us our debts, as we forgive our debtors." Verses 14,15 "For if ye forgive men their trespasses, your heavenly Father will also forgive you: But if ye forgive not men their trespasses, neither will your Father forgive your trespasses."

Matthew 18:21 "Then came Peter to him, and said, Lord, how oft shall my brother sin against me, and I forgive him? till seven times? Jesus saith unto him, I say not unto thee, Until seven times: but, Until seventy times seven." Also, notice Verses 23-35. (Mark 11:25, 26)

Engaging in continual repetitious repentance or constant questioning if we are bound is an unhealthy, unbalanced mindset. Condemnation is a trick of the enemy. It keeps us ashamed and only focused on our shortcomings. Without Jesus, we will always fall short. If you feel ashamed but cannot explain why, or if you still feel ashamed after repenting for the sin, that is a spirit of condemnation at work. God *convicts*, meaning He will let you know the sin so that you don't continue. 1 John 1:9 lets us know He forgives when we confess.

Therefore, remember that if it is a season of repentance, it is more of a pull to search yourself with an attitude of humility and sincerity. If you are about to step into a new level spiritually, it is not unusual to feel drawn into this season of repentance. Those are brier-exposing seasons.

When walking through the woods, often as a child, if I got too close to the edge of the path, I would often get delayed by a nearby brier attaching itself. My dad referred to those as "wait-a-minute vines." Delay doesn't always mean an attachment, but it is a common symptom of one. If you are feeling delayed in your spiritual progress, just consider that it might be a "brier."

CHAPTER 13
TRUE MERCY

True Mercy is Powerful:

I went through a challenging time to learn one of the most valuable lessons I've ever learned about what real forgiveness means.

I had been openly betrayed by someone I had trusted, who had become bitter toward me after a misunderstanding. At the same time, I then felt the same bitter feelings toward another in an ironically similar situation, although I kept my feelings hidden. Without realizing it, secretly in my heart, I was no different from my betrayer. I couldn't see that I was harboring the same feelings as the one who betrayed me until the Lord gave me a series of dreams.

In the first dream, God let me know that unless I was willing to rejoice for the one, I had bitter feelings against, instead of being bitter, I was no better than my betrayer. That was a bit of a tongue-twister! In the two dreams following that, I found myself protecting my betrayer against two attacks: an alligator first and then a water serpent. I stood between that person and their attacker in the authority of Jesus' Name, and the attacks were thwarted. In prayer the morning after the third dream, the Lord showed me that because of what my betrayer did against me, sin opened them up to attack, but I could step in spiritually and receive the attack in the place of my betrayer. I'm ashamed to say I hesitated for a second in prayer because I knew how significant an attack could be. I then entered intercession, feeling such a burden to stand in the gap, and take the attack, whatever it was going to be. Afterward, the Lord assured me that in my repentant state and because that situation had been directed against me, I had authority that my betrayer did not have over the attack. So, I prayed and rebuked the *voice* of the enemy. God showed me it was an attack by Leviathan, which I will mention more of later in this chapter. I then prayed for protection and covering over my betrayer, myself, and my family. In all of this, Jesus revealed to me the true definition of mercy and more understanding of what He did for us when He hung on the cross for our sins and took our place. It was a week or two before I saw the miraculous results of that prayer and was sobered by the seriousness of warfare.

The perfect timing of God is unmistakable. I immediately encountered a similar trial just after learning that important lesson on mercy. This time it was with someone in a place of leadership and spiritual authority. Hurt by a series of events, and after attempting to resolve it, I eventually asked God how spiritual leaders could get away with making decisions and hurting others with little regard for the long-term damage. God replied immediately and told me that those in authority are held to a higher standard and, therefore, are at greater risk spiritually if in sin. (James 3:1; Luke 12:47, 48) I felt the weight of this revelation and suddenly prayed for God's mercy on that person and their whole family.

Although it was a lot at once, it was not a coincidence that the previous issue happened just before this one. I was so thankful that the Lord showed me what true mercy and forgiveness were because, without that revelation, I could've easily responded incorrectly to each situation. We are to especially respect those in ministry and authority. (1 Samuel 24:5-7; 1 Chronicles 16:21, 22; Romans 13:1-8; 1 Timothy 2:1-4; Hebrews 13:17; 2 Peter 2:9-12) Submission is a critical component in obedience, but there is a balance, and those in authority answer to the Lord. It is not a small matter with the Lord if someone abuses authority.

How do we know if we have truly forgiven someone? It may take time to pray for them while asking for God's help. If we are willing to stand between the offender, and their possible attack, feeling compassion and concern for them and genuinely wanting the best for them, unforgiveness won't stay. That is true mercy. Remember the law of the harvest. We reap what we sow. It is in our best interest to sow mercy every time.

The bottom line is that God loves people and will do His best to reach them. I have known Christians who think that when someone is going through a tragedy or hardship, they are being punished. There are several instances of this happening in the Old Testament, so it is easy for that to be our default reasoning. However, I offer you the truth behind this, that *punishment* to people is usually a *pursuit* from God. Yes, God is just, and certain rules in the spirit realm allow legal rights for punishment because of sin, but God uses judgment as a pursuit. (The book of Jonah; Isaiah 48:10; Amos 4:6-11)

The Lord repeatedly tried to return Israel to Him through their captivities and judgments. Judgment is His last resort, and even today, He can use a prophet as He did in the account of Jonah. Time after time, idolatry was a legal right for the enemy to attack. It is also important to note that when judgment does happen, we are not to rejoice against those who have wronged us. (Proverbs 24:16-18; Ezekiel 36:2-5)

The Lord told me in prayer one day that I should be careful not to provoke others to sin. In Matthew 7:6, it says, "Give not that which is holy unto the dogs, neither cast ye your pearls before swine, lest they trample them under their feet, and turn again and rend you." If I use wisdom, I won't give a valuable thing to someone who doesn't know what to do with it. If I try to force my biblical understanding on someone who isn't ready or open to it, they could possibly speak against God's Word or mock me, and as a result, a judgment could follow because of the law of the harvest. It is wise for me to find common ground instead – be their friend, feel out where they are in their belief, and then begin by praying for mercy for that individual and that their eyes and ears will be opened to the Lord in a merciful way. Most people are familiar with Christianity and its common general values or standards, so verbally proving where we stand isn't *always* necessary. Biblical laws and rules are given for our *protection*, not as punishment, and if following rules, instead of getting to know the One Who created them is the only depth of our relationship with God, how shallow we will be. Also, the Judge must be righteous. If we attempt to judge others on this earth, we immediately become unrighteous in thinking we are righteous enough to judge. Judging and discerning are two different things. Discernment usually involves not knowing why you feel that way about the person and possibly questioning yourself. The Holy Spirit can confirm it. Judging inappropriately involves a self-righteous spirit.

While we are still in Matthew 7, I noticed something interesting in a warning about false prophets in Verse 16. That word "thorns," appears again. Is it my imagination, or does that word keep popping up? (Pun intended.) According to this scripture, thorns are the fruit of sin. Thorns are the invasive weeds that ruin our hedges of protection. (Proverbs 24:31)

Job – Leviathan:

Most are familiar with the Old Testament book of Job. His year made 2020 look like the best year ever! In an exchange between God and Satan in Job 1:6-12 and Job 2:1-6, something stood out to me in the Hebrew translation. It seems that God didn't just point Job out randomly, as I've always thought. The word "considered" in translation is a combination of two Hebrew words, 07760 *suwm* – *direct*[1] and 03820 *lev/leb* – *the heart*.[1] It seemed as if the Lord was asking Satan if he had his heart set on Job because it was evident in Job 1:10 that not only Satan knew who Job was, but he also knew of his prosperity. Maybe God had seen Satan searching Job's spiritual hedge for a crack. Interestingly, Satan, not a random demon, took this case upon himself.

It is easy to be uneasy about this story until you reach the end. Imagine the help this story has been since it was written!

After the tragedies, Job's friends appear on the scene in Job 2:12,13. They cried, tore what I hope was their least favorite mantle, and threw dust on their heads. They even sat silently on the ground with him for seven days and nights! That must have been protocol for Old Testament bestie status. A trivial thought here, but I wonder if they were eating or bathing during this week of silence? Those conditions didn't sound conducive to a good mood. Was it the discomfort of sitting on the ground? Was it the awkward silence combined with too much togetherness? I don't mean to make light of the situation, but the circumstances didn't appear comforting. It seems there was an absence of flowers, soft tissues, hugs, and warm fluffy blankets.

In Chapter 22:1-7, 9-11, 21-23, Eliphaz said some strong words that sounded like a misunderstanding had occurred. In my mind, I picture a 'gasp' during his speech. If there had been social media back then, I wonder how many of these guys would've been unfriended at least once through this process.

Then after many conversations had taken place, in Job 41, we find that God mentions a nightmare of a creature called Leviathan, described as a fire-breathing sea dragon/serpent.

God spent a whole chapter on the description and characteristics of Leviathan. If you've ever researched or experienced spiritual warfare, you will encounter what many refer to as the spirit of Leviathan. Sometimes literal enemies in the Bible are seen as spiritual enemies today, and no doubt that very spirit was behind the enemy in the Bible, too. For example, you might be familiar with Queen Jezebel, who first comes on the scene in 1 Kings 16:31. Then, her name reappears in Revelation 2:20. That same manipulative, seductive *spirit* against the prophetic that embodied Queen Jezebel made a comeback. As suggested before, evil spirits were originally created as immortal angels/spirits and did not die just because people did.

I don't think it was a coincidence that Leviathan was mentioned to Job at the end. Could it have been symbolic of a spirit or a principality behind the spiritual attacks Job had been facing? It is apparent that one of Leviathan's main attributes was pride, according to Job 41:34. Leviathan's most noticeable characteristics indicate him as one who twists, ignites with his mouth, is thick-skinned, has a heart of stone, and is feared. The scripture mentions mire and sharp stones in the mire. Not only does he cause you to be stuck, but he wounds his victims there. Verse 25 implies that his crushing causes the mighty to sin. It is a complete recipe for relationship division – misunderstandings and words that spread like fire and ignite tempers. Other characteristics include betrayal, breaking promises, refusing instruction, and being too proud to apologize or admit wrongdoing.

Just after this, Job, having seen a new revelation of God, repents in Job 42:6. In that verse, the word "myself" isn't necessarily there in Hebrew, and the word for "abhor," 03988 *maac/maas,* means *cast away or reject.*[1] It was an interesting discovery in light of the reject-renounce idea.

Who knows, maybe Job was being tried because he did everything right? Maybe God wanted to purify Job, or He just wanted Job to have a new revelation of Him. Perhaps it was similar to the children of Israel in Deuteronomy 8:2, 16, or in 2 Chronicles 32:30, 31 when God wanted to know what was in Hezekiah's heart. Whatever the reason, the sincerity of Job was commendable after all he had been through. That is where *religion* and *relationship* part ways. Sincere heartfelt repentance shows humility, genuineness, and sensitivity.

When I am in the powerful presence of the Most High God, His presence is humbling. It just feels natural to repent, no matter how good I have been – even my ability to do good was given to me by the Lord. (Our righteousness – Isaiah 64:6)

Several scriptures refer to righteousness as clothing or a covering garment: Job 29:14; Psalms 132: 9; Isaiah 61:10; Zechariah 3:4; Revelation 3:4, 5; 19:8

After Job repented, God was angry with three of Job's friends for their words. (Elihu from Job 32-36 isn't mentioned in this.) In Job 42:7-9, God instructs them to take their sacrifice to Job and ask him to pray for them. I find it interesting that God turned the captivity of Job when he *prayed* – 06419 <u>*palal*</u> – *interceded, intervened*[1] for his friends in Verse 10. Because their sinful words involved Job, it made sense that his prayer/intercession for them turned the tide. No doubt, Job prayed mercy upon his friends. When misunderstandings and accusations arise between friends, causing division, that same pattern of warfare happens, especially if it becomes public. If we have *truly repented*, the next step is to *intercede*, praying *mercy* for the offender in the relationship, binding the enemy from causing division, especially binding his *voice* and *words*. I have seen this work every time.

In the beginning, Job lost almost everything, and soon after, his health and relationships were also under attack. In the end, there's the fantastic fact that Job ended up with a greater revelation of God, an acknowledgment of the enemy or enemies that had attacked him, and double for his trouble, but let's focus on the mercy factor.

Mercy is mighty (Luke 6:27-38,) and if you consider the law of the harvest (Galatians 6:7-9; 2 Corinthians 9:6; James 2:12, 13), it is also crucial. Following are just a few notable scripture references about mercy in the New Testament:

Matthew 5:7 The merciful are blessed and will obtain mercy
Matthew 9:13; 12:7 Mercy and not sacrifice
Matthew 23:23 Weightier matters of the law
Luke 1 Mercy is mentioned at least five times in this chapter
Luke 10:36, 37 Examples of mercy
Romans 11:30-32; 15:9; Isaiah 11:10 Mercy for the Gentiles
Romans 12:8 How to show mercy (with cheerfulness)
2 Corinthians 4:1 An attitude of mercy (it is enlightening to search the word "mercy" in our Bible and see how often it was used and how it was the general attitude of the greatest heroes of faith.)
Ephesians 2:4 God is rich in mercy.
Titus 3:5 Not by works of righteousness (also note the uses of regeneration and renewing)
Hebrews 4:16 Come boldly unto the throne of grace
Hebrews 10:28 Without mercy
James 3:17 Wisdom from above full of mercy
James 5:11 Tender mercy
1 Peter 1:3 Abundant mercy

Mercy:
Hebrew "02617 _checed_ – *goodness, kindness, faithfulness*"[1]
07355 and 07356 _racham_ – *compassion, the womb, tender love,*[1] (I have heard the analogy of mercy in comparison to a womb protecting a fetus)
"03727 _kapporeth_ – *mercy seat, covering and place of atonement*"[1]

Greek 1653 _eleeo_,[1] 1656 _eleos_ – *help afflicted, kindness by divine grace*[1]

Other Mercy-Prayer Connections:
As mentioned earlier, if we pray according to our will or with impure motives, that is wrong. Praying your will on someone is a type of witchcraft and one way to pray amiss. For example, if you are praying for someone and do not agree with something they're doing, the correct response in prayer is for God's will and mercy in that situation. Pray they would be sensitive and obedient to God's voice. If this person is sinning, pray that God would mercifully give them revelation and that He would have compassion on them. Praying that God convicts someone for something that we think is a sin but isn't a proven sin, according to scripture, is *wrong*. Take inventory of your motives. If we are praying bad circumstances on someone, or our attitude toward the person we are praying for is wrong, these are wrong motives and similar to those who would attempt to cast a spell. Our judgments and prayers have a way of coming back to us.

When we crush our will, motives, and pride in prayer, that is a type of sacrifice. In my previous circumstances, I had repented of my grudge against the individual that had caused hurt, but I had to crush my will, feelings, and sense of being right and step into that place of intercession. God meets us when we bring a sincere sacrifice of a broken will, and our prayer, as incense, as seen in the Old Testament Tabernacle, can only burn when ignited with the coals of a true and repentant sacrifice. The incense was also a type of covering as the priest stepped into the Holy of Holies. I had asked God to reveal what each ingredient stood for in the incense formula. One evening I was researching it, and suddenly I saw a type and shadow for ingredients and coverings of acceptance in prayer.

Four elements in a recipe for appropriate covering in prayer:

Humility – Stacte – Clothed with humility – Humility gives God the glory.

Faith – Onycha – A garment of praise – Praise strengthens faith.

Sensitivity and Obedience – Galbanum – Beauty of holiness - Allows God's authority.

Pure Motives – Frankincense – Robe of righteousness – Keeps your will from ruling.

Trials can bring our flaws to the surface, like stirring cake batter with a spoon. It is a simple example, but so true. If He can trust us, God also wants to give us more authority and knowledge, which only comes through purification and experience. At times He reveals the lumps through situations so they become visible enough to be removed. Sometimes we only know what is in us once a problem happens to bring it to the surface. That situation wasn't the judgment of God; it was a method to purify us because that characteristic we had was not appropriate for the next level. That is why I cherish my revelation of mercy, I wouldn't have chosen to go through the situation, but I would never have gotten the depth of that revelation otherwise. In our journey into the more profound things of God, each new level seems to require more from us, but we cannot let fear of trials or failure deter us from reaching for MORE.

Our words are important, especially if we have a prophetic calling or are in a place of authority. (Numbers 14:27; Psalms 34:13; 39:1; 139:4; Proverbs 12:18; 15:4; 18:21; 21:23; Ecclesiastes 5:2 Isaiah 3:8; Matthew 5:22; 15:18; James 3:2-9; 5:12; Jude 1:8-10) Since God's Word speaks things into existence, if we have His Spirit living inside us, couldn't our words do similar things in the spirit realm, especially if we have a prophetic ministry? It also helps to remember that most people do not intentionally set out to say hurtful things. We all come from different backgrounds, and we communicate differently. The enemy loves to capitalize on misunderstandings.

What if, in the sense of a spiritual building, we are securing a support beam (a positive word or prayer) that would help our neighbor, but instead of reinforcing it, we take a sledgehammer and tear it down (with negative comments) without the realization that we are connected? We damage their wall without seeing that we are living on the other side of that wall. We can take another approach – standing in the gap, making up the hedge, and supporting our neighbor.

Love Should be our Foundation and Motive:

I went through a season before receiving an understanding of deliverance, where I spent most of my prayer time loving God. Sometimes I was a little concerned I wasn't covering the needs of friends and family, but I couldn't escape the overwhelming feeling of just loving Him. In Romans 13:8-10, Paul makes the point that love fulfills the law. In 1 Corinthians 13, he gives key information not only for every Christian believer in life but also for those who engage in spiritual warfare – the idea that every good deed is almost in vain if the people involved do not have love as their true motive – real agape, unconditional, love. That love originates in God; if we truly love God, we will love people. Even though we break His heart, He still loves us. His vulnerability is not a weakness. It's love. Jesus used His last breath to pray the prayer of mercy on those who crucified Him. Love is the proper foundation for a productive Spirit-filled relationship with Jesus. Love creates appropriate respect and reverence, not an unhealthy fear. If you received Jesus out of fear of going to hell, it is vital to balance your foundation with the true love of God. Furthermore, love is a balancing factor required in spiritual warfare and deliverance. Without love for God and people, ministry in those categories will be dangerously unbalanced.

Our true intentions, especially for those willing to fight in the spirit realm, must be gauged with respect, love, and mercy. We should maintain a healthy level of respect for everything God has created. We do not condone nor agree with the evil we encounter, but God alone is the Judge. Apart from Jesus, I can do nothing good. It is essential to give Him all glory because thankfulness puts us in the proper mindset and prevents us from having harmful attitudes. The spirit realm is no place for arrogance, self-righteousness, entitlement, or pride. If we can understand God's love for us and grow in our love for God, we will learn how to love people. Salvation and freedom of people are the heartbeats of God. The subject of deliverance must be handled with love and discernment. No one can be forced into more freedom. Sometimes the understanding just isn't there yet.

It is important to remember that someone's salvation is not our judgment. We cannot assume everyone needs deliverance from an evil attachment or is even open to understanding it at first. Unfortunately, despite the number of scripture references for evil spiritual attachments, many in our church still do not want to acknowledge that aspect of ministry. Since they have salvation, they might be comfortable and uninterested in the discomfort of *more*. Deliverance is not politically appealing or sophisticated. It does not belong to any one person – it is Jesus' ministry – so it belongs to every person. It is sometimes misunderstood and messy, but so was the cross.

CHAPTER 14
CHRISTIAN DELIVERANCE?

<u>Contradiction?</u>

You might still be unconvinced that a demonic attachment can remain inside your mind or flesh while also being a Holy Spirit-filled believer. (Holy Spirit-filled believer is defined as living a holy and separated life based on repentance of sins, baptism in Jesus' Name, and the infilling of the Holy Ghost with the evidence of speaking in other tongues.) I'm convinced that the Holy Spirit will come in and fill as much of us as is available. It is possible that many of us have dealt with these spirits in prayer and did not even understand what was happening. I do not believe that *every* evil attachment immediately leaves until they are *ordered* to leave, however. I have not found a scripture that states everyone is automatically delivered from everything once receiving the Holy Ghost. Sometimes we allow sin, such as unforgiveness, to linger, but the Lord is merciful to deal with us when we are ready to understand. I had many things to work on as a new believer, but God didn't expect me to be instantly perfect before and after His Spirit entered me. God loved us while we were sinners. The whole idea is that He is a merciful God trying to save and have a relationship with us because He loves us. How often has freedom been hindered, forcing someone to live a tormented or miserable life by struggling silently because they think what they are experiencing is normal?

The following scriptures are the ones usually quoted to dispute the idea that a demon can remain attached after someone receives the Holy Ghost:

<u>1 Corinthians 3:16, 17</u> "Know ye not that ye are the temple of God, and *that* the Spirit of God dwelleth in you? If any man defile the temple of God, him shall God destroy; for the temple of God is holy, which *temple* ye are."

The same Greek word is used for "defile" and "destroy" – 5351 <u>*phtheiro*</u> *– to shrivel, wither, spoil, ruin, or corrupt.*[1] These scriptures were written to the Corinthian church by Paul. Verses 1-3 indicate that those he addressed were carnal, with envy, strife, and divisions. Those conditions are corrupting and, if left alone, can cause our spiritual man to wither or shrivel.

<u>1 Corinthians 6:15-20</u> "Know ye not that your bodies are the members of Christ? shall I then take the members of Christ, and make *them* the members of an harlot? God forbid. What? know ye not that he which is joined to an harlot is one body? for two, saith he, shall be one flesh. But he that is joined unto the Lord is one spirit. Flee fornication. Every sin that a man doeth is without the body; but he that committeth fornication sinneth against his own body. What? know ye not that your body is the temple of the Holy Ghost *which is* in you, which ye have of God, and ye are not your own? For ye are bought with a price: therefore glorify God in your body, and in your spirit, which are God's."

1 Corinthians 10:20-22 "But I *say,* that the things which the Gentiles sacrifice, they sacrifice to devils, and not to God: and I would not that ye should have fellowship with devils. Ye cannot drink the cup of the Lord, and the cup of devils: ye cannot be partakers of the Lord's table, and of the table of devils. Do we provoke the Lord to jealousy? are we stronger than he?"

2 Corinthians 3:17 "Now the Lord is that Spirit: and where the Spirit of the Lord is, there is liberty."

2 Corinthians 6:14-17 Verse 14: "Be ye not unequally yoked together with unbelievers: for what fellowship hath righteousness with unrighteousness? and what communion hath light with darkness?"

The new Corinthian church had situations unique to an environment embracing gentile believers. Some might have been previous temple prostitutes in Corinth since Aphrodite worship was popular. That religion included fornication and sacrificial food in its worship. Christians were instructed to choose only a Christian mate for marriage and not to fornicate – joining themselves with unbelievers and idolaters. Today, it is common to see mixtures of Christianity and pagan practices where the advice of the previous scriptures are still relevant.

James 3:10-12 "Out of the same mouth proceedeth blessing and cursing. My brethren, these things ought not so to be. Doth a fountain send forth at the same place sweet *water* and bitter? Can the fig tree, my brethren, bear olive berries? either a vine, figs? so *can* no fountain both yield salt water and fresh."

These scriptures discussed the tongue and hurtful words of our mouths. Should true believers use the same mouth to praise God and curse others?

Matthew 6:24 "No man can serve two masters: for either he will hate the one, and love the other; or else he will hold to the one, and despise the other. Ye cannot serve God and mammon."

This scripture follows the verses mentioning, "The light of the body is the eye:" between Jesus' message on laying up treasures in heaven and "...seek ye first the kingdom of God...."

"Mammon" was translated from the Greek word 3126 *Mammonas* – otherwise defined as *treasure, riches, and wealth personified.*[1] If our hearts/minds are full of desire for earthly treasures instead of godly ones, our focus and attention are misplaced.

1 John 5:18 "We know that whosoever is born of God sinneth not; but he that is begotten of God keepeth {5083 *tereo – watch, guard, fortress, full military lines*}[1] himself, and that wicked one toucheth {680 *haptomai – to attach oneself to, touch*}[1] him not."

This last scripture reference does not mean we cannot sin after salvation. It means that a true born-again believer will not continue or remain in sin. This is evident from John's preceding verse in 1 John 1:8. How many of us have sinned after conversion? I'm not saying we must sin, but I am saying that corruption is possible. If we are proactive in watching and guarding ourselves after we are born again and delivered, and if we repent when we sin, we can be safe from the enemy's grasp of attachment. Notice the word "toucheth" used in 1 John 5:18 and its definition in Greek, confirming my word choice of "attachments."

Colossians 2:10-15 is sometimes used when debating the possibility of a Christian having attachments, also. The context seems to be concerning religious laws, traditions, and trespasses because literal and spiritual circumcision is mentioned.

John 8:36 "If the Son therefore shall make you free, ye shall be free indeed."

This verse is in the middle of Jesus addressing Abraham's seed as people who were in bondage to sin.

None of these scriptures refer to a Christian being off limits for an attack or attachment of the enemy. In fact, each group of scriptures was written to *believers*, giving instructions to eliminate and avoid sin.

I have also heard that the Holy Spirit and Satan cannot be in the same place. God is not afraid of Satan. If it is a matter of sin that prevents God's presence, how did He choose us in the first place? Romans 5:8

Job 1:6-12; 2:1-7 Satan appears before God.

Ecclesiastes 3:16 Judgment and wickedness; righteousness and iniquity in the same place

Zechariah 3:1-4 On the right hand of Joshua

Matthew 4:1-11 Jesus in the wilderness with the devil

Matthew 13:24-30 Wheat and tares together

Matthew 16:23 "...Get thee behind me, Satan..." (Interestingly, this is recorded just after Verses 18 and 19, in which Peter had just received the keys to the kingdom of heaven. And also after Matthew 10:1, when the disciples had been given power over unclean spirits.)

Mark 4:15 "...Satan cometh immediately, and taketh away the word that was sown in their hearts."

Luke 22:3, 31 "Then entered Satan into Judas...;" Also, Satan desired{1809 *exaiteomai – beg or demand*}[1] to sift {4617 *siniazo – shake to overthrow*}[1] Simon "as wheat:"

John 6:70 "Jesus answered them, Have not I chosen you twelve, and one of you is a devil?"

John 13:27 "And after the sop Satan entered into him. Then said Jesus unto him, That thou doest, do quickly." (speaking of Judas)

Acts 5:3 Satan filled the heart of Ananias.

Romans 7:21 "I find then a law, that, when I would do good, evil is present with me."

2 Corinthians 12:7 messenger of Satan to buffet

God is omnipresent:
Psalms 139:7-12 "Whither shall I go from thy spirit? or whither shall I flee from thy presence? If I ascend up into heaven, thou *art* there: if I make my bed in hell, behold, thou *art there. If* I take the wings of the morning, *and* dwell in the uttermost parts of the sea; Even there shall thy hand lead me, and thy right hand shall hold me. If I say, Surely the darkness shall cover me; even the night shall be light about me. Yea, the darkness hideth not from thee; but the night shineth as the day: the darkness and the light *are* both alike *to thee.*"

Jeremiah 23:24 "Can any hide himself in secret places that I shall not see him? saith the LORD. Do not I fill heaven and earth? saith the LORD."

Romans 8:38, 39 "For I am persuaded, that neither death, nor life, nor angels, nor principalities, nor powers, nor things present, nor things to come, Nor height, nor depth, nor any other creature, shall be able to separate us from the love of God, which is in Christ Jesus our Lord." (Underlined emphasis mine)

A Christian can allow envy and strife to become embedded inside their heart just as a thorn can work deeper into the flesh. If those sins remain, they become spiritual doorstops allowing openings for all sorts of evil possibilities:

James 3:14-16 "But if ye have bitter {4089 *pikros – piercing sharp*}[1] envying {2205 *zelos – zeal, jealousy, indignation*}[1] and strife {2052 *eritheia – self-seeking, intrigue, contention*}[1] in your hearts, glory not, and lie not against the truth. This wisdom descendeth not from above, but *is* earthly, sensual, devilish. For

<u>where envying and strife *is*, there *is* confusion and every evil work</u>." (Underlined emphasis mine)

That scripture *did not* say, "...for where envying and strife is, there is confusion and every evil work, *unless it's inside a Christian.*" Christians are not immune to feelings of envy and strife. It appears that envy and strife are directly connected to confusion and evil. Since human beings are usually the ones who feel envy and have strife, we can conclude that there is a conflict in thinking that wherever evil is, God will not be. If that were true, many of us would've never been able to become Christians, and then Christians could never be attacked. I have not found in scripture where demons automatically fled individuals just because Jesus was nearby or approached those individuals.

Every scripture that I've seen used for debate in the idea that a Holy Ghost-filled person cannot be demonized, has been taken out of context. That teaching destroys the possibility of more freedom and healing for whoever believes it. Battling an unclean spirit or generational curse does not make us any less saved. It can, however, make us miserable, and consider giving in to the lies if we let it remain. As humans, none of us have it all together or are above failure. If we are honest with ourselves, we can deal with our own issues and strongholds. This leaves less time to judge others.

CHAPTER 15
INTERCESSION

Intercession is linked closely to the deliverance ministry. An intercessor, through God's power, steps into next-level prayer. This is done by repairing a spiritual hedge or warding off an attack by standing in the gap. If we are sensitive as we grow in prayer, we can become intercessors for those in need. Intercession is usually a burden that comes over me unexplainably, and it seems I cannot quit praying until it lifts. Sometimes I know where, who, or what it is, and sometimes I do not. This is not to be mistaken for travail, which feels more physically intense for me and involves a spiritual birth of something like a ministry, a new season, or the spiritual birth of someone. Both intercessory prayer and travail seem to produce quick results. In my experience, I usually travail in relation to someone receiving the Holy Ghost, and I tend to feel intercession more for situations concerning other countries. If you have not yet encountered this type of prayer and would like to, try focusing on something the Lord has designed you to personally feel passionate about and let the Lord lead and guide you in prayer. If I'm honest, I'll admit I do not like being overwhelmed with sad feelings and burdens that can feel draining. I believe that is why many people avoid these types of prayers. However, if you want to experience God's extreme love and compassion, those overwhelming moments in prayer are just a tiny glimpse of God's feelings for others. If we don't pray these priceless prayers, who will? Who knows what God is doing in our lives and families as we stand in the gap for others?

Spiritual warfare and the spirit realm are very real. Intercessors are crucial to God's Kingdom. As several in the Bible stood between judgment and the person or persons, intercessors are still needed today. I have been blessed to travel to several beautiful countries, but intense intercession is my favorite place to be. Whether you are an intercessor who mostly intercedes for individuals, specific situations, worldwide governments, nations, or the unknown, you are NEEDED! Let God give you the words He wants to be spoken on earth as He has spoken in Heaven. (Proverbs 15:4)

Have you ever noticed the longer you are around someone, the more you pick up their attributes? There is no substitute for spending time in the presence of God in prayer.

Jesus is our ultimate intercessor. He took our place and gives us access to the throne. (Hebrews 4:14-16) In Isaiah 53:12, the *intercession* translation in Hebrew is 06293 *paga* – *entreaty, encounter, strike, attack, touch, boundary, impinge, to reach the mark*.[1] This is very similar to one of the translation definitions of *sin* – Greek 266 *hamartia* n.– *no share in, err, wander, miss the mark, mistaken*[1] */ 264* *hamartano* v.[1] and also in the Hebrew root *02398 chata – miss the mark, forfeit, miss the path*.[1]

Another intercessor example I study is Moses, who appeared before the Righteous judge on behalf of Israel when they sinned. (Deuteronomy 9; Psalms 106:23)

I picture intercession similar to a walled fortress that has been damaged by an attack. The intercessor steps into the damaged area, securing it, repairing breaches, and fighting off other attacks. Isaiah 58:12 is an awesome verse that gives added insight into the role of an intercessor.

CHAPTER 16
HOW TO ACHIEVE DELIVERANCE

I want to tell you that there is one standard formula for successful deliverance, but there isn't. Every situation is different. There are helpful principles, however, that require discernment and sensitivity from the Holy Spirit to navigate through the process.

Every child of God will, at some point, engage in spiritual warfare, and each believer can, through Jesus, be involved in deliverance. Still, everyone is not necessarily called into a deliverance ministry. Let me give an example from Acts 2:17. It states, "And it will come to pass in the last days, saith God, I will pour out of my Spirit upon all flesh: and your sons and your daughters shall prophesy..." (also it is repeated for the servants and handmaidens in Verse 18.) Everyone with the Holy Ghost has the potential to prophesy, but everyone does not have the title of a prophet. The same goes for intercessory prayer: Everyone can and should intercede, but everyone might not have the drive to flow in the ministry of an intercessor. If you do not feel a pull in the direction of deliverance, do not allow the enemy to bring condemnation or guilt.

I firmly believe that we are more effective if we work in the calling for which we were created. I've noticed there is usually a natural ability, excitement, passion, and a hunger for more in the particular area we are called. Don't let yourself become discouraged trying to fit into a place you were not created to flow. You are unique, and God created you to be effective in the ministry for which you were intended. There will be opposition, but peace always accompanies God's will.

Most Christians, especially leadership, often feel what I call *performance pressure*. We attempt to hide flaws to prevent others around us from either stumbling or judging us. It is a sacrifice to be vulnerable, but I remind myself that those who exploit someone else's struggles are really magnifying their own problems. If my testimony can bring freedom to one person, it was worth it.

In conclusion, let's discover, <u>*How* to accomplish deliverance. As we learned in Chapter 4, "Repentance," this can be done by removing the legal rights through repenting and renouncing sin. We continue further by commanding it to leave in Jesus' Name</u>. I greatly urge each Holy Ghost-filled believer to include renouncing with their repentance. Renouncing specific sins or flaws triggers unclean spirits that could be lurking and attached. Don't be afraid or surprised if something surfaces. Most of the time, this does not mean someone is "possessed" or controlled by Satan. If you are a child of Jesus, Satan does not own you. If you are patient and allow yourself to be led by the Holy Ghost, He will lead you through the deliverance, especially if you do not have access to an experienced deliverance minister.

Sometimes the deliverance can be lengthy, and a stubborn spirit may have to be commanded several times before it leaves. When Jesus encountered this in the stories of Legion, He asked its name. Legion didn't lie. Jesus' authority requires obedience. Also, asking why or if it has a legal right to be there could be helpful in this scenario. There could be unforgiveness or an unbroken curse. It may take time. If the legal rights are removed through repentance and renouncing, and the person wants it to leave, it will. Faith can also be a factor. Time spent in prayer and fasting can help this. (Matthew 17:17-21) Praise and scripture can benefit as well. In deliverance once, I felt to read a scripture about the specific sin that caused an attachment. Nothing had happened during repentance and renouncing, but a manifestation happened when the scripture was read. Because attachments are predominantly attached to our flesh, mind, or emotions, they often leave with a physical manifestation of some kind. Violence is also possible. Every spirit does not necessarily leave with a manifestation, however. Wisdom and discretion should be used. If the deliverance is planned, it would be wise to have help, a questionnaire, and a release form for them. If they are the opposite sex, another person of their gender should be there if possible. Physical contact is not necessary in most cases. Many times, Jesus just commanded the spirits to leave. Ask the Lord for discernment and the assistance of His angels if needed.

Communication with the individual experiencing deliverance is an important factor. If possible, ask the person what they feel or hear during the process. You can ask God to expose and reveal anything that might be there or lingering. If you are doing self-deliverance, do not get discouraged. That can be very draining. Refrain from feeling pressured to be delivered entirely all in one day. Maybe God wants to reveal some things through the process.

If you have not repented, been baptized in Jesus' Name, and received the Holy Ghost with the evidence of speaking in other tongues, it would be best to receive deliverance with an experienced Holy Ghost-filled believer because once the spirits leave, you need to fill that empty space with the Holy Ghost. It does no good to get delivered if you are not willing to follow Jesus. I know of ministers who prefer to do deliverance only on believers. However, some attachments can hinder the person from receiving the Holy Spirit.

It is possible to receive the Holy Ghost by yourself through seeking and surrendering to the Lord completely. As we look at Psalms 22:3, we see that praise and worship will turn the Lord's attention to us, so if there is ever any struggle to enter God's presence, sincere praise and worship are key. If you have been filled with God's Spirit at home, it is important to find an assembly of believers that teach Biblical truth so that you may grow and prosper in the Lord to reach and help others. Matthew 18:19, 20 – Unity is powerful.

Once again, I do not claim expertise in the subject of deliverance. My burden is to provide information through my experiences, research, and what the Lord has revealed so far, which is constantly growing.

The blood of Jesus is not anemic but powerful in that it can override our sins and lack of knowledge. His blood can embrace us in our sinful state and walk us out into freedom physically, emotionally, and spiritually. You can be free if you struggle with something, whether it's trauma, generational, or from your own doing.

I am providing an *example* of a prayer for deliverance. I chose to address the spirit of *fear* here, but you can replace each underlined word with what you are facing. This is just a template to help you get started.

Example of a Deliverance Prayer:

Lord, I thank You for Your love and mercy toward me. Your Name is above all names, and no one is more powerful than You. Jesus, I confess *fear*. I repent for and renounce *fear* and every sin that has given *fear* a legal right in me. I break all evil contracts and agreements I have made with *fear*, whether through my words, thoughts, or actions. In the Name of Jesus, I ask that You remove *fear* from my record. I rebuke and resist *fear* and declare it has no legal rights here anymore. Through the authority of the Word of God and in the power of Jesus' Name and His Blood, I command *fear* and every spirit under it to be bound together and leave me at once. I command it to go to the abyss and never to return in Jesus' Name. I ask for Holy Ghost *faith* to take its place.

(If you feel it could be a generational curse) - In Jesus' Name, I sincerely repent for and renounce every sin in the bloodline that would cause a curse of *fear* on me or my family. I ask that You remove this sin from our record and cover it with Your blood. In Jesus' Name, I break every generational covenant and contract with *fear*. I break every bloodline curse of *fear* and command it, all damages and every evil spirit associated with it, to leave me and my bloodline immediately and go to the abyss.

Just repeating a prayer is not the key to freedom. Be sincere, and <u>let the Holy Spirit lead you through deliverance</u>. Allow yourself to be sensitive to the Lord's voice. Ask the Lord for restoration and repair of the damage done. Also, remember to thank Jesus.

If I begin to exhibit signs of an attachment, such as continual nightmares or other obvious signs, as previously mentioned in Chapter 11, "The Where," I will address it in prayer. I have done this several times, and every time God has shown me if I am actually dealing with an attachment. Then I will ask God to reveal what it is and if there are more under its authority. I ask for God to lead me in my deliverance, and I also ask for Him to send angels to help me as I begin prayer, like the one I just mentioned. There have been only a few times that I didn't know the origin or exactly what it was. During those times, I repented for whatever brought that attachment into my life and broke all covenants with it.

The situation can be awkward or strange at first. The supernatural realm has many unknown variables, so it is crucial if you are helping an individual through deliverance to be discreet so that they do not feel judged about what they are experiencing. Remember, it is a spirit, not the person.

Jesus doesn't expect us to be superhumans; we can never be good enough to save ourselves, but He wants a relationship with us. As willing vessels, we must pour out the toxic, let Him clean us, fill us with the Holy Spirit in every area, and help us to be watchful so we can pour out to others. This is paramount to having a thriving relationship with Jesus. (Matthew 7:21-27)

If there were strongholds and habits created, it might take time to remove those altogether. Consistency and persistence are key to reaching complete demolition in a stronghold. Do not be discouraged by what you've been through. For me, overcoming the fortress and the habits that timidity built over the years has been an ongoing process. The invasive thoughts and nervousness are gone, but I will revert to that comfortable place of reserve if I'm not careful. If a stronghold exists, pushing forward and destroying the prison created is important. This will help prevent an attachment's return. Your victory might result in an attack from the enemy, so watch and pray against this while celebrating your new freedom! The follow-up process is just as necessary as deliverance. Do not let this crucial part of working against strongholds be neglected.

Suppose you do not require deliverance from attachments. In that case, you will likely encounter someone who does, and you will now be a soldier equipped with information to help pull them out of the thorn-piercing entanglement of captivity.

www.ingramcontent.com/pod-product-compliance
Lightning Source LLC
Chambersburg PA
CBHW060323050426
42449CB00011B/2621